T0116812

INSPIRING OTHERS TO INSPIRE OTHERS

Minimizing Conflict through Restorative Conferencing

Changing Lives through Changing Attitudes

Edna Fenceroy

WestBow
PRESS
A DIVISION OF THOMAS NELSON

ISBN: 978-1-4497-2243-2 (e)
ISBN: 978-1-4497-2241-8 (sc)
ISBN: 978-1-4497-2242-5 (hc)
Library of Congress Control Number: 2011912940

WestBow Press books may be ordered through booksellers or by contacting:

WestBow Press
A Division of Thomas Nelson
1663 Liberty Drive
Bloomington, IN 47403
www.westbowpress.com
1-(866) 928-1240

Printed in the United States of America

WestBow Press rev. date: 12/07/2011

Introduction

From the outset of this work, my desire was to leave something of worth to my family. However, due to my love for friends and others, after writing a few pages of this text, I realized it would be selfish and somewhat remiss of me to dedicate this writing only to my immediate family whom I am most grateful for help shaping my life as I am. I owe much to my deceased parents, Gus and Jane Thomas, who freely and patiently imparted their wisdom and values to me and who were my spiritual mentors.

I am thankful for my myriad of work experiences, and those who were part of these contexts. Our mutual and committed focus provided a foundation for structuring and developing my personal skills. I consider myself fortunate having served with so many extraordinarily skilled and caring people who offered me the platform to be exposed to the restorative work of conciliation. I am incredibly blessed for the skills acquired from these orientations. Using restorative conferencing to help others resolve their disputes by inspiring them to use the strength that is within them to correct what is in their power, helped my life to be transformed. The many encouraging comments received from clients regarding the positive impact of my work on their lives were inspirational in helping me to write this book. After a family conference with a mother and her sons, the mother stated, "We have been going to therapy for six months now and we have been helped more by your service in one hour." Bible-based curricular served to enhance my moral compass and direct my daily behavior. My academic background, experience, and the studying of God's Word, equipped me with the strength and fortitude to construct this work. I was greatly encouraged by this

Scripture: "So whether we eat or drink, whatever we do, do it all to the glory of God." (1 Corinthians 10:31).

I sincerely acknowledge the encouragement of friends and family consisting of biological kinship and in-laws who were ever present to offer me new challenges and insights into problem solving. The joy of my grandsons served to calm me and helped me to remain focused in order to write this book. Their gentle warm hugs and willingness to be coddled at anytime was a source of genuine comfort.

A special thanks to my dearly beloved husband whom I respect, love, trust and appreciate. His love, patience, prayers, and work helped sustain me spiritually, emotionally, and physically since the union of our marriage. A strong sense of gratitude goes to my two dear, loving sons and my caring daughters-in-law whose undoubting support challenged and encouraged me to do and be the best that I can. Most assuredly, I am eternally grateful to the clergy who guided my ecumenical path through teachings and examples.

I am humbled to dedicate and share this work with all of you. It is my desire that this writing provides some fundamental guidelines and core values for anyone seeking to live a peaceful life. It is God's will that we love Him and each other, and writing this book is my way of demonstrating and expressing my love for you. The word, *facilitator,* as used in the concept of restorative conferencing, does not limit your capacity to use its principles. This approach is comfortable for anyone who desires to use a structured and peaceful process to resolve a dispute.

As you read through this text, you will notice that the process is presented several times; this is to remind you of the various applications suited for restorative conferencing.

Edna Fenceroy

Preface

The principal purpose for writing this book is to present a comprehensive and precise alternative to resolving disputes. When conflict exists, meeting of the minds dissipate. Invisible walls are built and those concerned are looking to have their personal views prevail. It is the author's aim to provide an approach that is peaceful and less threatening than arbitration or litigation; and promotes living in harmony with others.

This writing not only focuses on providing an easy and alternative framework for resolving disputes by the practitioner, it also offers a guide for anyone who wishes to use a structured design for facilitating a conference at home, in schools, churches, and other social and public organizations. It sets an informal platform in order to benefit from an organized pattern that can help streamline a comfortable process for discussing issues, goals, and other matters.

The principles offered in this text encourage you to respect the views of others, even when you do not agree, and encourage an understanding that all people do not think alike. Therefore, the perceptions and viewpoints of others will at times not be consistent with our own. Generally perceptions and principles are based on personal experiences, core values and understanding. Recognizing that difference embraced with an attitude that it can be helpful rather than adversarial, will help lead to a more tolerable path of gaining an understanding of the dispute and each other. The restorative process is based on the biblical principle of doing unto others as you would have others do unto you.

Resolving conflict is more restorative and transformative when it is viewed as a process that offers opportunities to help ourselves and others rather than primarily focusing on gaining a resolution. Conflict offers the privilege of learning to know the other person involved in a dispute a little better. It offers opportunities for self-growth by understanding that others do not usually see us as we see ourselves. Learning to leave room for the opinions of others without judgment or condemnation is conducive to peacemaking. Understanding that perceptions are real to the person holding them, but are not necessarily factual, opens the door for finding facts and gaining a better understanding of what happened.

Conflict gives us the privilege of seeing ourselves as others see us. When involved in a conflict, it places a mirror in our face. It reveals our true being. How we see ourselves can determine how we deal with conflict. If you have the attitude that *nobody ever gives me anything,* or *everything I have, I personally worked hard to get it through my own efforts,* then you might not be willing to compromise to the point of reaching a mutual resolution even though you might be right to some degree. If you have such an attitude, you might ask yourself these questions: Do I work for the next breath that I breathe? Do I work for the privileges to feel, see, hear, taste, and smell? These are all precious gifts that help us to function in our daily lives. Helping others when it is in your power to do so is a biblically-based principle for living in harmony.

"Do not withhold good from those to whom it is due, when it is in your power to do it." (Proverbs 3:27). The stories shared in this book have been modified to protect the identities of the characters.

Seeing ourselves as others see us

Contents

"Blessed are the peacemakers,
for they will be called sons of God."
Matthew, 5:9 NIV

"Therefore, however you want people to treat you,
so treat them, for this is the Law and the Prophets"
(Matthew 12:7, the New American Standard Translation).

"As we have therefore opportunity, let us do good
unto all men, especially unto them who are the
household of faith" (Galatians 6:10).

RESTORATIVE CONFERENCING IS USED
TO CORRECT RATHER THAN PUNISH

CHAPTER ONE

The Power of Storytelling

The origin and power of storytelling began ages ago. In Africa, it was a source of reference for historical events and tribal history. It was a way of life. As understood by Leslie Marmon Silko, storytelling in Africa was not only for amusement, it was used for healing of the body and mind. Referenced in the "Epigraph *to Ceremony,*" 1977). Africans used storytelling as a verbalized record of history. Through conversations with descendants from my ancestors, I learned that stories were kept alive and remembered by repeating them from one generation to another.

Storytelling is an integral and crucial part of the restorative conferencing process. During this phase of the process, the participants have the opportunity to tell their own story and give their personal views of the dispute. A person's story is generally a personal perception about what and how something happened. Initially, an offender's view might be totally different from that of the other participants. After both parties have shared their stories, time is given for each party to be questioned by the other. After these discussions, additional information about the conflict is heard, and the participants often become more comfortable with discussing the conflict since they now have a better understanding of the other person's participation. Mutual resolutions are based on a clear understanding of the events and with an effort by all parties to work toward a common desired goal. Storytelling is important in conferencing because the disputants know that they are being heard. All parties are given uninterrupted time to tell their story the way that it is understood by them.

Jesus taught his disciples through storytelling and parables. The word *parable* is defined by some dictionaries as a short moral story. "Jesus spoke all these things to the crowd in parables; he did not say anything to them without using a parable. So was fulfilled what was spoken through the prophet: 'I will open my mouth in parables, I will utter things hidden since the creation of the world.'"

"With many similar parables, Jesus spoke the word to them, as much as they could understand. He did not say anything to them without using a parable. But when he was alone with his own disciples, he explained everything." (Mark 4:33–34).

The power of storytelling in the context of restorative conferencing and conciliation is evidenced by the challenge and insight it offers to its users, and by the altered behavior of those who told their stories. Storytelling has a unique role in conferencing by allowing the participants the opportunity of getting to know each other a little better. Hearing the perceptions of others, evaluating options, and giving grace by allowing the opponent to "save face", set the tone for the participants to be honest and straightforward in their dialogue. Storytelling challenges one to be open and truthful about a situation; it provides an opportunity for the parties to own their participation in a conflict or a success. Conferencing offers the privilege to display God's love and serve grace to others through recognition and encouragement, which are important elements in resolving conflict.

As a child, I can remember that, after coming home from school, completing assigned chores, and eating dinner, my siblings and I would sit around the wood-burning heater and listen to our parents tell us stories of their childhood and what it was like for them growing up in a completely segregated world. They shared with us the politics of that time and how my father paid a poll tax in order to vote. Both of our parents were Christians—my father was a minister—and both told us about the love of God. During that time, it would have been rare to hear a Christian giving you what is now called "steps to salvation." You were taught that you must accept Christ as your personal savior. At that time, these conversations were referred to as family talks or discussions. Ground rules were set for family living and activities. What is now referred to as core values was mentored to the family. This is not saying that parents did not error in those days, but there was a strong emphasis placed on doing what was right and attending church on Sundays.

Where does conflict start, and from where does it come? We know that the Bible teaches that the heart is desperately wicked. So then, we can know with confidence that sin is the root of conflict and all evil because conflict starts in the heart that is wicked. In this context, *heart* is not a reference to the organ but rather refers to the core or center of our human nature that is sinful. The Bible teaches that, "For all have sinned and fall short of the glory of God." (Romans 3:23). "What causes fights and quarrels among you? Don't they come from your desires that battle within you?" (James 4:1).

Conflict exists from a myriad of sources, mainly sin, which is a violation of God's law. Conflict is often viewed as a disturbance in a relationship, according to some dictionaries. I contend that conflict is not only derived from a relational focus, but also that discontentment or uncertainty of circumstances serves as a basis for conflict. I was once involved in a conversation with a young mother who wanted to purchase a home, but the type of home she desired was not within her budget. It could appear in this scenario that there was a conflict with finances. This conflict was more of an interest-based issue because the focus was on getting the mother's daughter into a good school. The young mother wanted a better neighborhood because she associated better schools with better neighborhoods. After long discussions and conferencing, the mother realized that her child was only six months old, and she decided that the area where the young mother was presently living was just the place she wanted to live at the time. Through conferencing, she understood that she was not ready for her child to be cared for outside the home, and decided after more dialogue that her child would be under her control most of the time for the next four to five years. This would give her the time needed to purchase an affordable home in her current area, and by the time the child was ready for school her financial position would be stronger to purchase her desired home. It all turned out to be a wise choice and investment. At the end of five years, conservatively thinking, and if the current market trends at that time stayed stable, selling her current home could provide her with a sufficient down payment for another home of her choice. This is an example of conflict with circumstances with an interest-based focus.

This book offers various applications to resolving conflict through conferencing with the aim of providing facilitators with alternative tools for small group discussions. Group conferencing will be further explored throughout this text.

Conflict is further known to exist when the real issue is not identified or recognized and less significant issues are being challenged, or when there are opposing views based on a miscommunication. A couple was married for fifteen years and was failing to live in peace with each other. Just about anything could or would start an argument. If the husband left a glass on the table rather than putting it in the dishwasher or the wife left a light on when leaving the bathroom, either action could precipitate a big argument. How simple would it be, if passing through your kitchen, to take a misplaced glass or plate and put it in the sink and wash it or just place it in the dishwasher? How difficult is it to flick a switch to turn off a bathroom or closet light? It was not difficult to sense that something more significant than leaving a light on or a glass left on a table was at the root of this disturbed relationship.

The content of the book is written with a focus on moral character and core values based on biblical principles, because appropriate and constructive values can help minimize conflict. The stories told in this book have been modified, and the names of characters have been changed unless when referencing another author's work.

Minimizing Conflict through Restorative Conferencing

Restorative conferencing offers alternative ways to finding peace amid confusion. Peacemaking is about allowing room for others to have their own thoughts or beliefs without judgment or condemnation. Getting a clear understanding of what happened or understanding how the dispute occurred initially is the first step in order to work toward a resolution. Personal, verbal attacks, using inflammatory words or inappropriate body language such as, the slamming of hands on a table or certain facial expressions are counterproductive acts that could halt a mutual resolution. Everybody does not always feel the same as we do regarding certain circumstances or situations, however, we can still show others respect by allowing them to have their differences without agreeing with their perceptions. Allowing others to have their own perceptions while being able to maintain our own beliefs is a form of giving grace. Creating a trusting atmosphere clears the path for positive discussion, fact-finding, and mending relationships.

Conflict does not have to be distasteful or hurtful. It provides opportunity for self-growth, to gain insight regarding the matter at hand. It gives us an opportunity to examine ourselves and the privilege of gaining a better understanding of the opposing views of the situation. Most importantly, conflict often shows us who we are. Oftentimes I have heard people say, "I was surprised at myself. I did not know I could get that angry." Or, "I have never done anything like this before—I must have snapped." Understanding that conflict with others can stem from a sea of reasons and various sources, it is wise to recognize the source of the conflict. The root of a conflict can originate from a general dislike for another person. Envy or jealousy can be the cause of conflict when it is not recognized in a timely manner.

Opposing perceptions have been the root cause for many conflicts. Perceptions are real, and the reality is sometimes painful. Keeping in mind that perceptions are not always factual gives room for discussion. When at odds with another's perceptions, refrain from making declarations without having factual information about the situation.

The restorative conferencing process creates an atmosphere of trust and openness and is conducive to gaining a better understanding of what really happened. Each person's perception is explored and sensitivity is given to each issue in order to arrive at a workable solution. Respecting others by allowing them room to have their own perceptions, gives opportunity to save face in the event the opposing party wishes to change his view. Allowing room for an offender to "save face", often inspires him or her to accept and acknowledge accountability and responsibility. It is important to realize that allowing room for the opinions of others is not necessarily giving approval of their actions, nor is it compromising your own beliefs. It has been my experience that people would rather correct their own mistakes than have corrections forced upon them. Giving grace is a form of showing empathy. You are placing yourself in the other person's position because this is what you would desire if placed in the same position.

During my practice of restorative conferencing, I have seen time after time, when victims offer grace and empathy to the offender, the offender often has a change of heart and puts forth effort to heal the harm. Restitution comes in various forms. Sometimes what is only being sought is a sincere apology or an acknowledgement by the offender that he or she is accepting accountability for his or her actions. The restorative approach is most effective when its principles become a way of life.

Saving face

Tips for Minimizing Conflict

When you are trying to resolve a dispute, whether it is with another person or about personal circumstances, ascertain as many facts as possible before making a judgment or a decision that you might regret later.

Do a self-evaluation to see if you have a clear mind and conscience about the issues.

You might ask yourself, "Am I happy with myself, my life, my finances, and my family matters?" Your answer to these questions might impact the way you resolve a conflict.

Start thinking of viable ways to help yourself make certain changes. You might want to do research on what you would like to change, or even seek professional and divine guidance in the matter of your concern.

How we view ourselves can determine how we deal with conflict. If you have an attitude that *nobody ever gives me anything so why should I help someone else, or I have worked hard for everything that I have without a helping hand from anyone, it could be difficult for you to reach a an equitable and peaceful resolution.* In a sense that might be true to some extent about no one giving you a helping hand; however, do you work to behold the beauty of nature? Do you work for peace of mind or do you work for the next step you take? Some people do. Do you work for God's mercy which is undeserved? Healthy living promotes strong bodies, but these are divine gifts necessary to help us in our daily lives.

Minimizing Conflict by Applying Alternative Thinking

Alternative thinking is another way to rethink or redirect your thoughts through a given situation that is more beneficial than thinking negatively or emotionally going through a hypothetical situation.

It has been said, "If you keep on thinking what you have always thought, you will just keep on getting what you have already gotten." So if you want to change your life, start changing the way you think. You can start by asking yourself, "Is there a better way for me to make a certain statement or judgment?" Before undertaking a task, ask, "Is there a better way that I can make this work than my first determination?"

The following scenarios will help you to understand and give you some idea as to how you can apply alternative thinking:

A woman is on her way to work and her car stops on the freeway. Here are two ways she can think about the situation. Once you understand how to apply alternative thinking, start creating your own scenarios from your personal life to apply the process.

Her first instinct or thought could be, *Oh! I am going to be late for work, and my boss will not like that.*

Alternative thinking: *Thank God I was able to pull over out of the traffic before someone could hit me.*

Now, I have to pay someone to tow my car.

Alternative thinking: *I am so fortunate to have towing service with my automobile insurance; I just hope I paid my premium. If not, today is my brother's off day and he has a big truck so he will help me.*

Just because I am a female, the mechanic is going to take advantage of me, and I am going to pay more, perhaps for something that I do not even need repairing at this time.

Alternative thinking: *You know if something has really gone wrong with my car, I want to know. Getting it repaired could save my life.*

Alternative thinking: *Considering all that has happened, it is cheaper to get my car repaired than buying a new one and having to make monthly payments.*

Applying alternative thinking is beneficial for remaining calm in a stressful situation. It not only minimizes the chance for a potential conflict, it reduces the negativity that can lead to emotional stress and nonproductive circumstances.

Using Core Values to Minimize Conflict

What are core values? Core values can be defined as a set of guidelines, boundaries, or moral tenets that you use to guide your actions, speech, and ideals. Each of us should define our moral compass based on truth. Our moral values should be based on a standard of truth, purity, and a power that is higher than our own.

In establishing our core values, we must think about what makes us who we are. What drives me to do or say the things that I do? What stops me from committing unlawful acts or causing harm to others? Why am I grieved when I am not truthful, or why is speaking the truth important to me? Generally these virtues are controlled by your core values.

Listed below are some personal commitments that should become part of your core values:

I am committed to speaking the truth.

I want to care about others as myself.

I am committed to being honest.

I am committed to not causing harm to others.

I am committed to treating others the way I wish to be treated.

I will not murder or unjustly take what does not belong to me.

I will be kind to others regardless of how they treat me.

I am committed to not spreading gossip.

I am committed to helping others when it is in my power to do so.

I am committed to living a life that will not bring me or my loved ones to shame.

I will serve humanity with love and care. When you allow your core values to stop you for committing an offense or a moral violation, you have just avoided bringing self-inflicted conflict into your life.

A Sweet Marriage Gone Sour

The names Robert and Rita Russell will serve for the husband and wife. Rita was an exceptional decorator and housekeeper. Robert (Robert will also referred to as Bob) a loving, dedicated, and hardworking husband and father. They both were avid churchgoers. However, Robert fell short in his housekeeping and being tidy. Robert's failure to meet Rita's expectations in housekeeping incensed her over the years. She had talked to Robert about how she felt and how important maintaining a clean home was to her.

For the last ten years, both Rita and Robert would come home from work with virtually no conversation with each other unless it was argumentative. The marriage had begun to deteriorate. While visiting with them one evening, sitting in their living room, Rita started telling me about Robert's habits, and Robert started telling about Rita's habits. Not having a clear understanding of what was happening since both were talking at the same time, I asked if someone could please help me to understand what was being said or what both were trying to tell me. They apologized and asked if I would discuss their relationship with them. After both agreed to certain fundamental guidelines for discussion, such as common courtesy for each other while being engaged in a discussion, I agreed to hear their story.

Rita told her story concerning Robert's lack of housekeeping skills, and Robert told his story regarding Rita's lack of intimacy with him. After hearing their stories, it was easy to determine that this was an interest-based conflict. As their stories unfolded, what once was a happy marriage turned into an indifferent and bitter relationship. There was no socializing with other couples, which was a bi-monthly activity during the early years of their marriage, and happiness had turned into virtually a dislike for each other.

After the storytelling had begun, both Robert and Rita understood the benefit of having structured guidelines to facilitate their session. The benefit of establishing guidelines set boundaries for participation. The aim of structuring is not so much for limiting what is said or done, but it offers mutual consent to engage in dialogue that otherwise could prove counterproductive. If one party is not prepared or desires to discuss a painful or sensitive issue, the parties might delay or table that particular issue for a future time. However for this scenario the parties agreed to be open and frank about issues with the understanding that anything said would be kept confidential and not later discussed or mentioned again in order to hold the other party responsible for some prior demeanor or statement.

After the opening statement, Rita finally acknowledged to Robert that after his son came to live with them about ten years ago she no longer had him to herself. And now she was doing double the work around the house. Rita reassured her husband that she did not dislike Todd, but she was not happy about the way he was brought into the family. No family meeting was held in order to set boundaries and guidelines for the family to live in harmony. Robert's son just appeared one day without prior notice to Rita. Robert was aware that Todd was not getting along very well with his mother, but he never suspected that she would send him to live with Rita and himself. Robert understood Rita's concern and agreed to help out more in keeping the home clean and tidy. He apologized to her regarding the way his son came to live with them and admitted he had little idea how Rita was feeling about the situation. Robert's son was from a prior relationship with a different person before knowing Rita.

An Anger-Infused Marriage

As Robert was telling his story, he told of an angry and bitter wife. After several years of marriage, the relationship with Rita started turning sour. After coming home from work, there was constant bickering and nagging. Rita was angry with just about everything Bob said or did. According to Bob, Rita would come home complaining his income was not sufficient to sustain the lifestyle she wanted. Rita wanted to take lavish vacations, attend expensive social events, and wear high-end, name-brand clothes. Rita interrupted Bob by saying, "What's wrong with wanting to look nice when I go to work or attend an evening event?" Bob contended that Rita enjoyed expensive cars, jewelry, and eating at fine, upscale restaurants. He further shared how angry Rita would become when he tried to discourage eating out so often rather than cooking at home sometimes. They were spending close to one-third of their income on eating out and Rita's personal items. Debts were filling up the credit cards to capacity. Robert explained how incensed and livid Rita would become if he or Todd left an empty glass on the countertop after having a glass of water, or how angry she would become by not turning out a light after leaving a room. In spite of Rita's spending habits, it was difficult for Robert to understand the severity of leaving a glass on the countertop or table.

Anger had taken over Rita's personality. She wanted to give up her job in order to stay home and keep house. Rita wanted to experience the life of living like a queen, as told by Robert. Rita even complained of his social skills. Rita contended that she just wanted her husband to be the best he could possibly be. Initially Rita had the responsibility of paying bills, but that was taken over by Robert after she overextended the allowable credit amount on a couple of credit cards. Rita took money designated for paying bills and purchased expensive handbags, makeup, and jewelry.

Robert continued his story by telling Rita that all he wanted was to be able to come home to a peaceful and comfortable environment.

After Robert explained how his anxiety and feelings distanced him from Rita due do her lack of concern and intimacy with him, he reiterated his love for her and his desire to make things better. Rita proclaimed that she also wanted to make things better and acknowledged her addiction to anger. She was asked if she could help us understand how she became addicted to being angry. Rita shared that she enjoyed being angry and could even feel her emotions rising to the point of wanting to be explosive. Rita enjoyed being angry because she felt that would bring some discomfort to Robert or she would at least get an emotional reaction from him. At certain times, she enjoyed demeaning her husband and speaking negatively of him. Rita stated that she had given thought of seeking professional help regarding her anger, but, after deciding to use her faith and accepting Bible-based conferencing from her pastor, along with consistent Bible study, she felt that she could get it under control. After hearing her acknowledgment, Robert was pleased, and agreed to join her in Bible study and conferencing sessions. They both decided to engage in family devotions that would include Robert's son. Robert further encouraged Rita to seek professional or medical help and assured her of his support.

After a little probing into Rita's anger, she shared how she even pondered the thought as to why she was angry at Robert. She concluded that she recognized that it was not just her husband with whom she was angry, it was being angry at herself. She confided that she was not happy with her job and how she now sees the benefit of preparing for a job that would allow her to earn enough money to sustain a certain style of living. Rita discussed her errors and failure to prepare herself sufficiently for the future. While in school, she did not see the value of graduating from college or gaining the appropriate skills to propel her into a lucrative career. Her anger toward Robert was rooted in her own failure to be all that she could be, and she felt it necessary to try to make Robert be all that she wanted him to be. Rita wanted to live a lucrative lifestyle vicariously through her husband.

Rita's acknowledgment and recognition of her own inadequacies gave her insight into helping their son, Todd, to be the best he could be. They got involved in credit counseling and arranged a plan to pay off their debts. As a couple, they decided how much of their income would go toward setting aside funds for Todd's education. Rita stated that she now realized that a person had to position him or herself for challenges and new opportunities.

Both Rita and Robert agreed to have dialogue with Todd *together* in order to reassure their desire to have him as part of the family. Robert stated that he would talk with Todd about house responsibilities and assisting Rita with house chores and other requests for assistance when needed. They both admitted that the glass left on the table and not turning out the lights had anything to do with the deterioration of their marriage, however, it took a painful and hurtful relationship to bring them to recognize that it was time to take action to save their marriage by taking steps to enhance their relationship. Robert and Rita realized that their relationship or lack thereof, had to be addressed in order for them to gain a better understanding of each other and reestablish new guidelines for living in harmony in a peaceful environment. Rita asked Robert to forgive her for demeaning him with negative words by defaming his personal worth and demeaning his social skills. Robert accepted her apology and assured her that she was forgiven.

Using the restorative approach for dispute resolution, allows the participants to engage in honest and straightforward discussions. Remaining aware that whatever is said or done in a marriage conference is to work toward mending the relationship and not to tear each other down, both Robert and Rita were able to commit to an order of corrective measures that would lead them to a more peaceful and loving marriage.

Restorative Practice and Principles

Within the framework of restorative conferencing and discipline, restorative practice could be defined as the application of restorative principles steeped in moral values and biblical tenets. The focus is to help the offender take ownership of a behavior and make amends where necessary, and to enhance the offender's belief system in moral behavior.

I have practiced restorative principles for many years in my own life and have benefited from its applications, and inspired clients to be self-empowered by recognizing their own inner strengths. The positive impact displayed in peoples' attitudes as they engage in a restorative conferencing session are easily noticed as they use their inner strength to understand their own conflict. People generally respond in a positive way when treated with genuine respect and kindness.

The restorative conciliation process offers the opportunity for pre-conferencing with the disputants in order to familiarize them about the process. During the pre-conferencing phase, the conferencing process is explained, giving the parties a clear understanding of what to expect. Pre-conferencing is not always necessary when both parties are willing to participate without prior orientation. If a party is reluctant or requires extra information in order to feel comfortable with the process, pre-conferencing should be considered. Generally pre-conferencing is held with each part separately. However, if both parties agree, the pre-conference could be held with both parties present. When a dispute involves family members, pre-conferencing works well when both parties are present. The parties understand that only the process will be discussed.

During a pre-conferencing session when both parties are present, the parties might decide that they would like to enter into the conferencing phrase since both parties are available. This is permissible if the timing is convenient for everybody including the facilitator. If this should happen and everybody is prepared to proceed, the facilitator may start the process by giving an opening statement followed by other elements of the process offered in this text.

Applications of Restorative Conferencing

The applications of restorative conferencing are far-reaching. It is appropriate for groups of various orientations—civil, community, church, home, and organizations. The atmosphere should be one of relaxed bodies and attitudes. Often, participants are positioned in a circle. This places everyone on the same level physically, but it can also create psychological equality, because a circular position is less threatening than a rectangular table or desk where it can be assumed that the person seated in the chair "at the head of the table" has an edge of authority. A semicircle serves just as well for people in a relational dispute.

The aim of restorative conciliation and conferencing is to encourage and inspire self-empowerment of the participants to resolve their dispute through enlightenment and recognition. The facilitator manages the conference by keeping the parties focused on the impact of the offense while respecting each other's perceptions. The facilitator further seeks to understand what is in the best interest of the parties through probing and voluntary purging by the participants. The process encourages the participants to be honest and straightforward when disclosing or sharing information.

It is not the aim of this process to try to force anyone to admit or submit to anything not decided by him or herself. This orientation works best when the participants desire to treat each other fairly. The participants should come with an open mind and heart seeking healing or relief from the hurt and harm caused by the offense.

The confidentiality element of the process gives some degree of security that what is said in the session will remain confidential. Confidentiality brings a certain amount of comfortableness and trust to the process. The rule of confidentiality does not apply if anyone should make a statement that is perceived as a threat, or if anyone should admit to an unlawful offense punishable by law.

My involvement with the local Restorative Justice Department Community Conferencing Program solidified my passion to help others through encouragement, recognition, and accountability. The focus of restorative conciliation and conferencing is quite similar to the procedure of community conferencing. The tiered process of discussing the claim, examining the impact, and repairing the harm of community conferencing is often appealing to both the victim and the offender. This process allows both parties to participate in the process of righting a wrong. In order for this process to be effective, the offender agrees to be accountable for carrying out and following through with the agreed-upon remedy and resolution.

Restorative Conferencing

Restorative conferencing offers a process whereby an impartial third party, a facilitator, works with the participants to try to help them reach a mutual and desired resolution. Generally it is voluntary and less adversarial and expensive than litigation.

The process is informal, and the facilitator remains neutral at all times, while seeking to encourage accountability and ownership from all parties. The role of the facilitator is to ask relevant, open-ended, nonthreatening questions that solicit candid dialogue from the participants. The facilitator should look for small acts of kindness or willingness on the part of the disputants to work toward a resolution in order to offer earned and sincere recognition.

Fundamentals of Restorative Conferencing for the Facilitator

Listening Skills

A facilitator must practice good listening skills. You might hear what is not completely being said, or a party might interject something verbally in a very low voice that is important while another party is talking; thereby, not pushing the issue to be openly heard or addressed through meaningful dialogue. This means that when a facilitator hears a party using a low voice or interjecting a statement while someone else is talking, a prudent facilitator will revisit that concern. Restating or reframing what was thought to be said or heard gives time for discussion of the issue, thereby exploring the significance of the statement while giving recognition to the participant.

Eye Contact

When a facilitator makes pleasant eye contact with all parties— especially the one who is speaking—it helps validate their presence. It lets them know that what they are saying is being heard. Eye contact is also beneficial for the facilitator; it allows him or her to observe the speaker's demeanor and provides the opportunity to observe body language.

Body Language

Body language is a nonverbal communication that expresses our emotions and gives signals of approval, no approval, or a neutral attitude.

Body language is an important part of communication which can constitute much of what is being communicated. If you wish to communicate well, it makes sense to understand how you should not use your body to convey what you are saying.

Body language can be misinterpreted or misunderstood. For instance, a nod of the head might indicate you are in agreement with what someone has said; on the other hand, it could be understood as a ploy to deceive especially if it is accompanied by certain facial expressions. A nod of the head accompanied by a smirk on the lips could cause a misinterpretation of what is said.

Forms of Body Language

The slamming of hands on a table: Indicates anger, disagreement or frustration.

A frown: Expresses anger

Folded arms: Can express not being open to listening, a form of dismissal.

Raised and frowned eyebrows: A form of unbelief or unawareness.

A relaxed body: Indicates a willingness to listen.

A nod: Could indicate agreement (unless deception is involved).

A smile: Could indicate approval (unless deception is involved).

Civil Conferencing and Conciliation

Conferencing offers an alternative for conciliation and more direct approaches to disputes. Mediation is widely used for civil and court-mandated cases. Highly charged attitudes are often displayed in such cases, because the nature of litigation is often adversarial. Conferencing is useful for relational cases (whether court mandated or chosen by the facilitator or participants), because it is less confrontational than a substantive approach. Conferencing also produces an environment that helps participants relax and feel comfortable with exploring both their feelings.

Many times when mediating a court-mandated case, the facilitator is not in a position to use discretionary seating; in these cases, make use of what is available. I remember facilitating a court-mandated case that involved a lease between a church and the church's landlord. Due to the demeanor of the involved participants, I decided to use the conferencing approach. It worked well because of the relaxed atmosphere, the opportunity to explore a workable solution and to identify issues, and the opportunity to talk about how the participants were impacted. Through this process, the relationship began to mend, and the air was opened for mutual and casual conversation.

Community Conferencing

Community conferencing is becoming more widespread for use in municipalities that are exploring alternatives to better serve victims and offenders guilty of nonviolent and nonsexual offenses. Municipal officials refer these types of cases to the District Attorney's Office and other law facilities for conferencing as an alternative to an initial jail sentence. The referral process is sometimes known as a diversion program. Diversion programs use community conferencing to give individuals who have committed offenses severe enough to receive a jail sentence not only an opportunity to heal the harm but also to become a better person by altering their behavior toward a more appropriate and positive way of life. It offers benefits to offenders if they comply with the terms to heal the harm. The violation is often deleted from their record with full compliance to satisfy the remedy.

In certain cities, people who partner with this entity of community service are trained to participate in conferencing with the victim and offender through a local Restorative Justice Program. When the conference convenes, generally the victim, the offender, and the community participants are all present. In the event the victim is not in attendance, the offender will often still meet with the group. This platform provides the offender and the victim with the elements of the three or four-tiered process described below. (The process might be modified or taken in reverse manner, depending upon the purpose or aim of the resolution.) This approach mirrors the restorative conferencing process in general ways; it is non-threatening, and the participants are treated with kindness and concern by the facilitator.

Tier One: Introductions and Icebreakers

After a brief introduction of the participants via some unique icebreaker, the facilitator gives an opening statement explaining the process. The offender is given an opportunity to share his opinion as to what happened. Questions are allowed from the victim and other members of the group, and the offender is given uninterrupted time to respond. The victim, if present, is given an opportunity to respond to the offender and offer his or her perception of the offense. The victim also entertains questions and comments from the group members and the offender.

Tier Two: Discussing the Impact

The group—including the victim and offender—talk about the impact this offense had on the victim, the offender, the families of both parties, and the community. This dialog is conducted in a very restorative and transformative manner. Even when the offender is being questioned and the group seeks to see the offender take ownership of his or her actions, encouragement and recognition are the focus of the intent. Tongue-lashing and finger-pointing are deemed unprofitable.

Exploring the impact of the offense from the various aspects is very powerful, as the offender comes to realize how his offense has impacted not only his own life and family but also the lives of the victim, the victim's family, and community members. The offender does not always realize the implications of misguided actions. The idea of the true cost of certain actions (such as theft and vandalism) might not even register with the offender at the time of the crime. If careful thought were given to certain crimes, the offender would realize that the results of his action could be very costly. Most of the time, the offenders have not considered how they personally will be viewed by friends, family, coworkers, and classmates. Immature offenders have rarely thought about how their behavior will impact their chances of future employment.

In severe cases when offenders are unsuccessful in completing the restorative process, a felony might be placed on their record, expanding the implications and impact of future employment opportunities. Usually, it is during tier two that the offender becomes straightforward with his actions and is able to express remorse and to indicate a willingness to make amends. Very often, I have witnessed the offender apologize and express remorse when given the first opportunity to speak.

Tier Three: Discuss the Issues of Restitution

During this time, the dialogue is focused on appropriate restitution for the victim. By a consensus of all group participants, a decision is made for restitution that must be mutually acceptable to the victim and the offender. Generally relevant aspects, such as time constraints, the ability of the offender to make amends, and the most effective and efficient manner to right the wrong, are considered in bringing about a resolution.

Tier Four: Discuss Accountability and Settlement Assignment

The fourth element of the process is often used to follow up with the restitution progress to offer encouragement or offer sources of support to the offender in order to complete the process in a satisfactory manner. When a student is the offender and is trying to make amends, and he or she is placed in a summer job, if the restitution is not complete, helping the offender to find other work could be explored in order to fulfill the assignment for healing the harm. If the offender fails to comply with the terms of restitution, a provision for consequences must be adopted to assure an equitable restitution.

Interpretations

The interpretation of community conferencing is viewed in several ways. Some see it as a second chance process to help offenders of nonsexual and nonviolent crimes to avoid jail time or a permanently scarred record. Others view it as a new paradigm in the context of restorative justice, and it is further viewed as an opportunity that allows both the victim and offender to participate in the restitution process. This process helps both the victim and the offender. The victim gets a chance for a face-to-face conference with the offender. It helps the victim because he receives an inside view of who the offender is and what was going through his mind at the time of the crime. The offender benefits because he has the opportunity to right a wrong and to make atonement.

Homework Assignment

Write a brief summary of this chapter, listing the principles and procedures taught in the text, being as specific as possible.

State how you personally plan to use some of the principles in your own life when facing a similar situation or other issues.

If you are involved in a group study, consider sharing your summary with other group members for discussion purposes.

Write a letter or prayer thanking God for what you have learned and how certain information has personally helped you.

CHAPTER TWO

Home and Family Conferencing

For many years, families have gathered at the kitchen or dining table for dinner. Families will often take this time to talk about what is happening in the home, school, church, community, and lives of each other. Household rules or guidelines are discussed, negotiated, and established for use and order in the home. Chores are defined and delegated as suited for each member.

The dinner table is the place where an array of topics is open for discussion. All family members are part of these discussions and have the liberty to change the focus of any conversation at any given time. This type of informal setting offers wonderful opportunities to engage in the elements of conferencing. It provides an opportunity to create an environment that, while still casual and informal, can become more organized with a specific focus. Home conferencing can be structured to follow the same process of a more formal setting where the participants are less familiar with each other.

Elements of Home Conferencing

A need must be identified for the conferencing. Has one family member violated a house rule? Has a need developed to discuss a certain issue or value? It is important to review moral values of a family even when there is no disturbance present. This is conducive to a friendly discussion without the aspect of judgment of another's attitude or behavior being called into accountability. Has one household member been offended by another member? These are all possible reasons to have a home conference.

Establish the appropriate facilitator. Usually one or both parents, the head of a household, or any other capable member deemed acceptable by the family can serve as the facilitator.

Establish an organized structure for discussion. An organized structure would include an opening statement from the facilitator as to why the conference is being called.

Discuss the guidelines for discussion. Talk about the confidentiality of what is being said. Discuss what has happened, the reason for the conferencing, and the desired outcome. If restitution is desired, encourage accountability and ways of making amends by the offender.

Discuss how the issue has impacted each family member.

Encourage forgiveness.

Reiterate family values and moral conduct.

Discuss and agree on how any harm done might be corrected.

Discuss accountability to right the wrong caused by the offender.

Conclude with a prayer of thanksgiving and a request for guidance and forgiveness.

Extending the Home Conferencing Process

The strength of conferencing is within the context and intent of the participants and the agreement if reached. Conferencing is voluntary, confidential, and encourages the meeting of minds and wills. Not only issues should be explored and considered but also interests. At times, an interest can be a stronger driving force than an issue. This concept should be kept in mind when striving for a mutual resolution for certain issues. When collective dialogue is heard and a mutual resolution is reached, this becomes an agreement (a willingness by both parties to abide its terms). This works well when each party understands the desires of the other. Using agreements as a rule or regulation can cause division when taken out of context. If one party violates a term of the agreement, try working it out together in a restorative manner before attempting more aggressive action. Conferencing promotes a win, win resolution because both parties must agree upon whatever the remedy might be. It can be generally assumed that when both parties willingly enter into an agreement, it is because this is what it takes to give both parties some resolve. It is important to remain aware that conferencing is voluntary and should be without undue pressure on either party to rush toward a resolution.

Making Conferencing Applicable to Friendships

When there is only one parent in the home, home conferencing can be extended to include other relatives or trusted friends. Close friends might find this process helpful by combining both families for certain conferences, especially when there are children of similar ages with common situations. Using this scenario, both parents will serve as facilitators: a primary and a co-facilitator following the pre-described pattern.

Children often embrace the values of close and faithful relatives and friends. In one-parent homes, the children might say, "I hear this all the time from mamma." However if a trusted friend or another relative is invited to the conferencing session along with their children of similar age, this could strengthen the impact of both parents' values when both share consistent views and attitudes.

Block Conferencing

Block or neighborhood conferencing could be useful when parents in the block or neighborhood come together for a common good of looking out for each other and promoting the welfare of the neighborhood. A community conferencing committee might be formed to deal with things happening within the community or certain items needed for the community. This process offers an opportunity to get local officials involved by inviting them to the conferencing sessions. The local police department could be invited to share their concern for the community and enlighten the members of ways to improve their community.

Homework Assignment

Write a brief summary of this chapter, listing the principles and procedures taught in the text, being as specific as possible.

State how you personally plan to use some of the principles in your own life when facing a similar situation or other issues.

If you are involved in a group study, consider sharing your summary with other group members for discussion purposes.

Write a letter or prayer thanking God for what you have learned and how certain information has personally helped you.

CHAPTER THREE

Restorative Conferencing
for Church Discipline

*"Brothers, if someone is caught in a sin, you who are spiritual
should restore him gently" (Galatians 6:1 NIV).*

For a long time, it has been the practice of some denominations
to discipline by bringing a member before an open congregation,
at large, with the member making a public statement of the
transgression and asking forgiveness from the church. Too often,
this action is all the action that is taken with little or no period
of active restoration. Restorative discipline offers an alternative to
this type of correction. It provides a conferencing platform and
discussions that are confidential and less public, with the aim of
accomplishing accountability, a repentant heart by the transgressor,
and an immediate restorative process.

Oftentimes, restoration begins right in the conferencing session. The transgressor gets the privilege of telling his or her story to a few church officials with strict confidentiality. This process generates an atmosphere that is nonthreatening and that is conducive for honest dialogue. It is the genuine concern and brotherly love provided by the participants that help the transgressor to be openly honest, accept ownership of his action, and seeks forgiveness.

"Brothers, if someone is caught in a sin, you who are spiritual should restore him gently" (Galatians 6:1).

"He who conceals his sins does not prosper, but whoever confesses and renounces them finds mercy" (Proverbs 28:13).

"If your brother sins against you, go and show him his fault, just between the two of you. If he listens to you, you have won your brother over. But if he will not listen, take one or two others along, so that every matter may be established by the testimony of two or three witnesses. If he refuses to listen to them tell it to the church; and if he refuses to listen even to the church, treat him as you would a pagan or a tax collector" (Matthew 18:15–17).

Suggested Format for Church Conferencing

A small group works well in conferencing. Since churches vary with their form of discipline, structure, and doctrine, the size of the conferencing group could be structured or modified for this context. Depending on the priority or severity for the conferencing, a different group size might be used for different purposes. Due to the secure and confidential atmosphere that is sought, it is suggested that small groups seem to be appropriate and more useful than large groups when using conferencing for corrective purposes.

Every format is customized to suit an organization's purpose and goals. It is necessary for each facilitator to construct his or her own opening statement, making sure that certain elements are included. Conferencing can be used for a myriad of circumstances, such as business meetings, especially where voting or ballots are considered, planning, reorganization, staffing, and structuring. The following format is offered as a guideline for group conferencing and may be modified to the needs of the participants. This guideline is useful for various discussions and could be useful for other orientations and facilitations.

During the conferencing process for church discipline, the facilitator should express that the participants dialogue and behavior should be guided by biblical principles. Since church discipline might require extra empathy and sensitivity, it is important to discern what is more appropriate, conferencing with one party at a time, or having them both present and the same time. Careful consideration must be given before bringing the offender and victim together. It is significant for the victim to know that the offender is held accountable for any personal violations or trust. However, initially, conferencing with each party separately offers the parties an opportunity to express their transgressions privately and before God.

Pre-conferencing sessions can help the participants to be better prepared for collective conferencing sessions. Pre-conferencing in private sessions with church officials gives the facilitators the privilege to offer suggestions for appropriate behavior and dialogue between the parties during a joint session. During the combined session with both parties present, facilitators may call for a private caucus if the parties' discussion becomes too sensitive or inappropriate. Embarrassing a participant unnecessarily is counter-productive to mutual resolutions. If the facilitators see a need to caucus with one party, the other party should also be caucused.

General Format

>   Opening prayer
>
>   Introductions of participants
>
>   Purpose for the conferencing
>
>   Definie the facilitator's role
>
>   Opening statement (include ground rules and elements of the
>   process)

In certain Bible based conciliation or conferencing, an expected outcome might also be suggested.

Open the floor for discussion

Discuss issues or interests that brought you to the conference

Discuss ways to heal the harm

State the desired outcome

Write a settlement agreement and terms for compliance

Adjourn with a closing prayer

Homework Assignment

Write a brief summary of this chapter, listing the principles and procedures taught in the text, being as specific as possible.

State how you plan to use some of the principles in your own life when facing a similar situation or other issues.

If you are involved in a group study, consider sharing your summary with other group members for discussion purposes.

Write a letter or prayer thanking God for what you have learned and how certain information has personally helped you.

If you are involved in a church discipline study, consider facilitating a mocked conferencing session in order to get a feel for what you would do in reality.

CHAPTER FOUR

The Restorative Conciliation Process

Conciliation can be described as a form of mediation, which is a process where an impartial third party works with the disputants and tries to help them resolve their own conflict by determining and reaching a mutual resolution. The facilitator has the neither power nor authority to render a decision. The aim of conciliation is to inspire the participants to use their own inner strength and moral values through encouragement, recognition, and sincere validation in order to reach their own resolution. The facilitator should stay mindful of promoting goodwill and fairness in order to help enable the disputants to overcome distrust and adversarial attitudes. Whatever is said in a conference or conciliation session should be kept strictly confidential. The exceptions to this rule would be if someone makes a threat to bring harm to one of the participants, including the facilitator, admits to harming a child, or admits to something that would be a violation of the law.

Pledging confidentiality to the participants helps pave the way for trust and honesty by the disputants. In conciliation, the participants retain the power to render their own mutual resolution. If no monetary restitution is required, the platform and elements of conciliation offer a wonderful and peaceful way to mend relationships, to make apologies, to ask forgiveness, and to get to know the other person somewhat better. This process is conducive for open dialogue and questions. Usually facts are distinguished from perceptions during open conversation. Open dialogue is necessary and important in helping the disputants to understand what is real in their minds, but it just might not be factual. Since we cannot determine with 100 percent accuracy as to what thoughts are in another's heart or mind, allowing each party the opportunity to explore and evaluate the issue can often lead to a clearer understanding with an enlightened perception.

Organizing the Conferencing Process

All parties to the dispute should be available.

Determine an accommodating location, one that is easily accessible.

Select a quiet, comfortable room that will eliminate outside interference.

A room with a round or circular conference table would be ideal for seating purposes.

Select a mutual date and time for the meeting.

Introductions

Introduce yourself and the co-facilitator if there is one.

Explain and define the conciliation process.

State your role as the facilitator.

If useful to do so, state the desired goal of the conciliation.

In a Church Setting

If the facilitation takes place in a church, and this is a dispute between members, a clear understanding of the process is helpful in setting a peaceful atmosphere.

Plan Your Opening Statement

An opening statement should discuss the guidelines for the session.

The benefit of confidentiality should be discussed. The significance of a written agreement should be explained. For instance, it should be discussed whether a written agreement is binding or not binding.

Discuss the ways that the dispute will be disposed, whether it is by a statement of no agreement, a complete or a partial withdrawal, or a written settlement agreement. In the event of a partial agreement, the portion that was not resolved should be discussed as to how both parties wish to proceed. A new drafted dispute could be agreed upon for further conferencing to consider the unresolved items or issues.

Personalize your opening statement to suit the situation.

Open the Floor for Dialogue

Give parties ample time to tell their stories and answer questions.

Obtain mutual agreement on any other guideline or benefit. For example, in a church conference, if one party wants each participant to be guided by biblical principles, all parties should be in agreement with this request.

Discuss Ways to heal the harm
Discuss Appropriate Restitution

An agreement should state who, what and when for a resolution to be effective.

Adjournment

Thank the disputants for their willingness to participate.

Discuss follow-up activity, if any.

Close with a prayer of thanksgiving.

Distribution of Settlement

Give each person a copy of the resolution or settlement.

Remind parties of the terms of the resolution and time lines, if any.

Conflict in Marriage

Too often conflict in marriages can be traced to poor communication or no communication. Many times couples have shared that there are just some things that cannot be discussed in their marriage. One wife revealed that every time the subject of money comes up, her husband would clam up and refuse to talk about their finances. The husband's refusal to talk about money initiated a big argument. Another spouse revealed that past issues of mistrust in their marriage kept them from having a loving relationship. Over the years, many stories regarding issues too difficult and painful for discussion between spouses have been the root of various disputes.

After several conversations with certain spouses, the manner in how the sensitive issues would come to attention was not at the best time, and sometimes not the right place. A young lady, whom I had met earlier knew approximately how long I had been married, once asked me how I had successfully managed to keep my marriage together. I shared with her that I personally believe it is an "ART" to maintaining a happy marriage. The acronym, "ART", meaning adoration, respect and love, the absence of any one of these virtues leaves a devastating void in a couple's life. Respect and trust without love are not complete within themselves to survive longevity in a marriage. Without love in a marriage, couples begin to fall out of love when intimacy decreases or cease to exist. A loveless marriage soon allows insignificant issues to become primary sources of conflict. Conversely, respect and love or trust and love alone cannot secure a happy marriage. The three virtues mentioned, love, respect and trust, are the staple that binds a successful marriage.

Timing is essential to a meaningful discussion of sensitive or stressful issues. Knowing how and when to discuss such issues play a key role in even being able to gain enough attention from both spouses to consider any type of helpful dialogue. Without the use of a facilitator, the following tips will help a couple to initiate the process of getting meaningful conversation with each other in order to give some time and attention to certain difficult subjects:

Pick a time when there is peace and calmness in the relationship.

Make known to the other spouse that you are troubled or need a better understanding on a specific issue.

Ask your spouse if he or she would be willing to have a conversation regarding a particular issue.

Indicate a willingness to discuss the situation when the other is ready.

Allow the other spouse to participate in determining the time and place for the discussion.

If asked what the issue is about, be as gentle as possible. Confirm that you believe this would be something that is beneficial to the marriage.

The purpose of the meeting and dialogue should be to improve communication and build each other up and not to deconstruct or point fingers of blame.

If a conversation is granted for discussion, agree to set guidelines.

Have a brief prayer before discussion, asking God to guide you and to give you the wisdom and love to understand each other.

Encourage straightforwardness and honesty.

Each party should be able to tell his or her story without interruptions or with a polite interruption by permission.

Agree not to hold what is said against the other spouse and not to bring up again anything that was discussed. If the discussion was not finished, agree upon another time and date to complete the discussion (this must be agreed upon by both parties). If this is not determined appropriate for a given situation such as if infidelity is admitted, postponing the discussion might be appropriate if emotions become highly charged. In such case, discuss seeking appropriate counseling before committing to another discussion just between the two of you. The purpose of the discussion should be to get a better insight on an issue, circumstance, or even to gain a better understanding of each other.

Agree not to use inflammatory words or profanity.

Oftentimes, during such dialogue between spouses, emotions are displayed; therefore be sensitive to the emotions of each other.

Offering forgiveness and asking forgiveness help in mending relationships.

Conclude in a prayer of thanksgiving.

Replacing New Year's Resolutions with Restorative Conferencing

A good time to establish specific times for discussion of certain issues is at the beginning of the year. Rather than making unrealistic New Year resolutions, call a family meeting to set goals and establish core values for the household. It is a great way and time to establish monthly or quarterly meetings just for the discussion of issues or situations that need attention. This time might be used for family discussions or used for both spouses to discuss marital issues. Taking time to acknowledge the contributions of family members is an important step in family bonding and growing closer together. This type of conferencing promotes confidence, self-empowerment, and validation of each member.

When it is difficult to agree during times of anger and dissatisfaction, if you have previously established a time to have such discussion then it is easy to just remind the other family members that this can be discussed at your scheduled time for family discussions. The pre-arranged time helps pave the way for continued conversation even when one party is reluctant to talk about a certain issue. Careful consideration should be given for guidelines when establishing family discussions at the start of a new year or just from the outset of making arrangement for such dialogue. Christians should be mindful of scriptural guidelines regarding family living. When couples' lives are guided by biblical principles, it should be understood what is acceptable and what is not. Holding one accountable for unacceptable behavior is much easier and acceptable when boundaries and guidelines have been previously agreed upon as a standard of living.

Family conferencing can be held at any agreeable time. Time might be set aside to encourage each other or to acknowledge and recognize the efforts of family members. It is so important to remember to have discussions to praise each other for his or her loyalty, love, respect, and trust of family members. Everyone enjoys recognition and words of appreciation.

What does the Bible say About Marriage?

God ordained marriage between man and woman, "And the Lord said, 'It is not good that man should be alone; I will make him a helper comparable to him." Genesis, 2:18. "Therefore, a man shall leave his father and mother and be joined to his wife, and they shall become one flesh."

Scripture instructs our children to be obedient to Him and to authority, "Children, obey your parents in the Lord, for this is right. Honor your father and mother,' which is the first commandment with a promise.'" Ephesians, 6:1–2.

"Wives, submit to your own husbands as to the Lord. 'For the husband is head of the wife, as also Christ is head of the church;

and He is the Savior of the body.'" Ephesians, 5:22-23. People have interpreted this scripture in various ways. The Scripture is not saying that the husband is more important than the wife; however, when the two are of the same mind based on biblical principles, it is easy to agree with one another. When the husband is practicing Godly behavior and supporting his household as a husband should do, the wife should have reason to be in agreement. The word *submit* as used in Scripture in this instance could be used as being in agreement with each other. The use of the word in this context does not mean that the wife should be enslaved or subservient. The wife should be appreciated and loved by her husband, and both should show respect and affection for each other.

Speaking the truth in love

Speaking the truth in love is a form of "serving grace." The Bible teaches that 'a kind word turns away wrath.' So give careful attention to not only the words you speak but also to the tone of voice used. "But speaking the truth in love, we will in all things grow up into him who is the Head, that is, Christ." (Ephesians, 4:15) Using inflammatory and unkind words is counterproductive to having a loving and trusting relationship. Constructive correction is best offered at the appropriate time. During a disagreeable discussion is not the best time to offer corrections. Correction is best served when a healthy relationship exists. When a conversation becomes too heated or emotional, to the point of one or both parties showing anger, consider politely ending the conversation by disengaging in further dialogue. This sometimes can help calm the situation and give the parties time to rethink a certain situation and get refocused. As a Christian, "You, however, are controlled not by the sinful nature but by the Spirit, if the Spirit of God lives in you. And if anyone does not have the Spirit of Christ, he does not belong to Christ" (Romans, 8:9).

Homework Assignment

Write a brief summary of this chapter, listing the principles and procedures taught in the text, being as specific as possible.

State how you plan to use some of the principles in your own life when facing similar situations or other issues.

If you are involved in a group study, consider sharing your summary with other group members for discussion purposes.

Write a letter or prayer thanking God for what you have learned and how certain information has personally helped you.

BUILDING PEACEFUL NEIGHBORHOODS

CHAPTER FIVE

Conferencing for Neighborhoods

Applying Restorative Conferencing to Neighborhoods

Initially, participants should ascertain a true description and physical layout of a particular neighborhood. Once this information is at hand, two or more community members should work toward discussing restorative conferencing with small groups to determine if it will be a good or suitable fit for the community at issue. If enough interest in the conferencing format is voiced by members present, this could be a good time to invite more members to be introduced to the process. It is important that the initial facilitators have a clear understanding of the process and some indication as to the implications it might have on the community.

Place of Meeting

Selecting a place for the first meeting is very significant because community members should feel that it is collective and with a concerted effort by the community to work toward a common good. With this in mind, securing a public location, such as your community library, a church, or some other public site for your meetings, would be conducive to community spirit.

Initial Agenda

Introductions of the facilitators

Introductions of members

A clear introduction of the process

Questions and answer period

How can this process have a meaningful impact in your neighborhood?

Discuss known or potential problems in the neighborhood and how this process could be used to ease or remedy the situations.

If enough interest is demonstrated, schedule another meeting to determine who will facilitate the next meetings and how facilitation will be handled. Determine how your program will be structured and solicit volunteers to assist with the work.

Suggested Applications for Community Restorative Conferencing

School issues

Community traffic

Community schools compared to other area schools

Pride in homeownership

Crime and theft

Activities for after school

Senior activities

Block watch

Any community concerns

Loud music

Playgrounds

<u>Restorative conferencing in one-on-one relationships</u>

Exercising the restorative conferencing process in personal lives is a viable and peaceful way to strengthen relationships. Using the prescribed process that might be modified to suit just two or more persons provides an opportunity to previously set guidelines or to predetermine how conflict will be handled in a marriage or in families of three or more.

After the disputants in a dispute have not been able resolve the issues, the claimant or the respondent will initiate the process by asking for a conference to talk about the issues involved. Once the conference is agreed upon, the participants should be given a pre-conference for the purpose of introducing them to the process and the expectations of each. At the time of conferencing, the participants should be prepared to talk candidly and courteously to each other with the hope of reaching a mutual solution. Starting the dialogue with complimentary politeness is useful when offered with sincerity and genuineness.

Generally people enjoy being recognized for something good or a worthy deed that they have done or accomplished. Taking time to thank someone for a kind act, or reminding someone how much he or she is appreciated for using the conferencing process, can be the staple that allows the process to work. Something as simple as putting gas in a spouse's automobile or preparing a favorite meal just to please the other person can go far in building a better relationship. Often when couples are involved in the conferencing process, they learn things about each other that they had not recognized or noticed prior to conferencing. Many spouses have acknowledged that it is not always about big issues and satisfying material desires but things that are often considered small and insignificant, such as just being able to say "I am sorry," which demonstrates humility. Being rude and having an unthankful and judgmental attitude can be useless in mending relations.

Homework Assignment

Write a brief summary of this chapter, listing the principal procedures taught in the text, being as specific as possible.

State how you plan to use some of the principles in your own life when facing a similar situation or other issues.

If you are involved in a group study, consider sharing your summary with other group members for discussion purposes.

Write a letter or prayer thanking God for what you have learned and how certain information has personally helped you.

CHAPTER SIX

Restorative Conferencing as a Preventive Measure

"He must turn from evil and do good; he must seek peace and pursue it. For the eyes of the Lord are on the righteous and his ears are attentive to their prayer, but the face of the Lord is against those who do evil" (1ˢᵗ Peter, 3:11-12) NIV.

Circular or group conferencing is not always suitable for some offenses, especially if the offense is of a violent or criminal nature. In this context, an offense is generally handled by the legal system. Using conferencing as a preventive measure works well when the process is structured to encompass the purpose of being preventive. The process of restorative conferencing works well when it is allowed to work by a willingness of the participants to cooperate. Self-entitlements and rigid attitudes along with a spirit of self-righteousness are counterproductive when using this process. Under certain circumstances, one-on-one conferencing is effective when seeking help for a personal issue. This being the case, confidentiality is very important when serving as a confidant.

Robert and Rita Russell, whom we met earlier, decided to use conferencing as a preventive measure as a way to get a head start on potential problematic areas of their marriage. Whenever a new offense was noted in the news, whether it happened at school or in the city, Bob and Rita agreed to privately discuss the matter first between themselves to evaluate the significance of the offense and determine if this would be a subject for a family discussion.

Using this scenario—the suicide at a local university and a shooting at a local high school—Bob and Rita would call a family conference, including their son after determining that this is something that the family should talk about since there were two children in the home; a niece who had come to live with them. In family conferencing, the setting is casual and is usually held in the comfort of the home. Both parents when present would facilitate the discussion.

The discussion is usually started by the parents stating what happened and how they were impacted by the news. Each child is given the opportunity to state how he or she was impacted by the news and how each felt others, such as the offender's family as well as the victim's family, were affected. They discussed what teachers had said about the event at school. All of this ado provided the Russell's an opportunity to probe the children's thoughts and to encourage them to communicate with them any problems that they were experiencing. They even asked their son, who is now in high school, if he ever had thoughts of harming anyone. Each child was given an opportunity to share how the offender could have handled the situation differently. Nina, the niece in junior high, shared her thoughts by expressing the sadness and hurt caused by the crime. The parents also shared their thoughts on how the offender could have avoided this event by reaching out and communicating with others who were in positions to help.

The aim of the Russell's was to discuss the current event at hand, but they also seized the moment to probe for anything that might be happening in the lives of Todd and Nina.

Indirect Probing

As demonstrated by the Russell's, indirect probing is when you can address a personal question or concern directed to a specific person by attaching it to a third situation in context. This type of probing lessens the personal impact of *saving face* by giving grace, and is less threatening than calling a conference to address specifically a particular party's action. In essence, you are addressing a particular personal issue by using a third party as the involved participant.

A Preventive Measure for Future Events

The Russell's' home conference offered opportunity to discuss the upcoming prom. Challenging scenarios may be created to stimulate the minds of students who might be planning upcoming events, such as going to the prom. Questions include who will be accompanying you to the prom? Where will you go after the prom, and how many will be riding in the car? Other questions may be these: How would you handle a situation where the driver has had too much to drink? What if the original agreed plans changed and you do not like the new plans your group has decided upon; how would you handle this situation? Asking questions of this sort will help people to think about how they might handle a particular situation if it should occur.

Such questions are important to know but need to be asked at the right time and place in the best atmosphere. The restorative conciliation and conferencing process is best served with willing and voluntary participation involving nonviolent issues. The court systems are better suited to remedy severe and violent offenses.

Homework Assignment

Write a brief summary of this chapter, listing the principles and procedures taught in the text, being as specific as possible.

State how you plan to use some of the principles in your own life when facing a similar situation or other issues.

If you are involved in a group study, consider sharing your summary with other group members for discussion purposes.

Write a letter or prayer thanking God for what you have learned and how certain information has personally helped you.

"Each of you should look not only to your own interests, but also to the interest of others" (Philippians 2:4, NIV).

CHAPTER SEVEN

Detailed Steps to Restorative Conferencing

Restorative conferencing is to help the participants to recognize and acknowledge any wrongdoing personally committed. The healing process can begin when one realizes the seriousness and impact of his actions and is willing to make amends. The facilitator should probe to learn the offense or what triggered the offender to commit such actions. Once the offender is able to consciously and willingly acknowledge that he understands what he did was inappropriate and is willing to accept responsibility, the facilitator is now ready to implement other elements of the process.

<u>Steps to Restorative Conferencing</u>

Opening statement by the facilitator

Introductions

Discuss the agreement to conference

Hearing the offender's story

Hearing the victim's story

Hearing comments from other impacted participants

Discovering how to repair the harm

Arriving at a settlement agreement

The facilitator's opening statement should explain the process of restorative conciliation and the role of the facilitator. It is imperative that the core principles of the process are made known during the opening statement.

Confidentiality

> The process is voluntary.

> The exception to the confidentiality rule is in the event someone makes a physical threat to another person or the admission of any abuse to a child, elder, or any other person. The facilitator must report such offenses to the appropriate authority.

> The participants may bring another person along for moral support or representation.

> A settlement agreement is mutually established and agreed upon by both the victim and the offender and should spell out the terms of compliance. It is for the purpose of identifying how the harm will be repaired. The agreement should state who, what, and when a certain issue will be satisfied.

> The settlement agreement should be in writing.

Introductions

After the facilitator makes a personal introduction, time is given to allow the other participants to introduce themselves.

Agreement to Conference

The facilitator should read the Agreement to Conference and ask if all the participants understand and agree to the agreement. The participants may approve the agreement with their signatures.

Hearing the offender's story

The offender will tell his or her story according to personal perceptions. If the victim wishes to tell what happened first, this is allowable by the consensus of the participants. It is important for the facilitator to keep in mind at all times that the process is about what is best for the victim and offender. It is about inspiring the parties to empower themselves by both recognizing *and* using the power that is within them in order to assist them in arriving at a mutual and viable agreement. In order to keep pace and stay in the moment with the parties, it might be necessary for the facilitator to take notes. All notes except the agreement should be destroyed after the conference.

Hearing the victim's story

Each party will be given ample time to tell his or her story according to his or her own perception. The facilitator should ask open-ended questions to discover how the harm impacted others, especially the victim, and the family members of both parties, if present.

Seek accountability from the offender

Acknowledgment and ownership of accountability of the offender's personal actions play a significant role in repairing the harm. Oftentimes an apology or some action of remorse will help validate the victim's claim. When an offender is unable to accept responsibility or acknowledge any participation in the offense, participants become stuck until someone is able to recognize that perhaps all the facts have not been disclosed. Relying on perceptions or hearsay is a hindrance to reconciliation and usually ends with an impasse.

It is essential to bear in mind that mistakes can be made. In the event that an alleged offender has been misidentified or wrongly accused while seeking to determine the facts and truth to a claim, it is just as important to render justice to the alleged offender with no less intensity as was granted the victim.

Comments from others impacted by the offense

Other participants may share their comments on how the offense impacted their lives or lives of others. Other participants may also offer suggestions for remedying the harm done by the offender.

Determine how the harm will be repaired

During the discovery step of the process, both parties will explore and evaluate options for settlement purposes. While repairing the harm is a significant aspect of this process, the aim is to help restore the damage caused to the victim and the offender. The process is aimed at helping the victim to feel good about the process and the outcome, and the offender is able to make better choices in life in both attitude and behavior.

The settlement

The settlement should be at the approval of both victim and offender. The settlement should be structured to identify who will do what and when. Generally this process works well because, rather than being a mandate by an arbitrator or judge, it is an agreement crafted by and between the disputants based on their willingness and commitment to remedy the conflict.

Homework Assignment

Write a brief summary of this chapter, listing the principles and procedures taught in the text, being as specific as possible.

State how you plan to use some of the principles in your own life when facing a similar situation or other issues.

If you are involved in a study group, consider sharing your summary with other group members for discussion purposes.

Write a letter or prayer thanking God for what you have learned and how certain information has personally helped you.

RESTORING HARMONY IN DIFFICULT SITUATIONS

CHAPTER EIGHT

Applying Restorative Conferencing to Facilitate Difficult Situations

During the past several years, I have encountered a growing number of cases that might be called opposing views or difficult people with rigid opinions. People demonstrating strong opinions or stiff-collared attitudes might even be perceived as being resistant to change. It is better to view opposition as an opportunity to gain a better understanding of the opposing party and of the issues, such as what happened and how it happened, rather than sticking to a preconceived perception without having all the facts. Opposition offers an opportunity to help the opposing party to understand you better, thus giving the privilege of being able to help each other. Disputes often serve as a mirror for people to see themselves as others see them. Seeing yourself as others see you can lead to a life-altering change particularly if you do not like what you see.

People generally feel good about themselves and how they behave without considering what others think. You might have heard somebody say, "I am a perfectionist," by what standard is he judging himself? Is his standard of measure based on his perceptions? Selling property is an excellent example of how you get several different views from the same experience. Being a real estate broker for many years, it has been my experience that a property is worth what a willing and able buyer is willing to pay, and not so much as what the owner wants to receive as proceeds from the sale. Several different views impact the sale of a property. First, you have the seller's view of what a property is worth, which sometimes even reflects the owner's personal sentimental values. Next, you have the buyer's view that is often based upon what potential value the property will have in the future. The buyer's first concerns are if the property is worth the asking price and if the property suits a current need. Afterward, the appraiser makes an opinion of the estimated value of the home based upon other sales and the homogeneity with other homes in the area. Do not forget the lender has its unique view of what a property is worth, taking into consideration the climate of the neighborhood, the location and condition of the property. These are all interest-based issues based upon needs, desires, estimates, and perceptions.

How we appraise ourselves is usually different from how others see us. With this understanding, it will help us to recognize that others might see us based on how they see themselves. Opposition helps us to look at ourselves and examine the judgment held by others. Opposition might be viewed as a medium that offers a platform that can be used as a springboard to help all concerned to bounce forward rather than to remain in a stalemate. We can all learn from each other and learn more about ourselves. Putting ourselves in the position of others helps us to be able to see through the eyes of others.

When conferencing so-called difficult issues with unyielding people, *look for ways to encourage the participants; do not concentrate on pinning someone to the wall or backing them into a corner; offer an escape to save face, and yet accomplish the desired purpose of reaching a mutual agreement.*

Providing an environment of trust and comfort

Confidentiality should be stressed when engaging in open dialogue.

Recognition helps one to have a sense of comfort.

Impartiality helps build trust.

Encouragement helps create mutual respect.

In this particular case, a mother named Catherine Clay had invited me to conference with her and her two daughters: Susan and Renita. Both daughters along with their mother arrived for the conferencing together. The mother was eager to get started but had some reservation because she did not know exactly how the younger daughter would respond. Renita, the younger, was the principal reason for the mother requesting a conference. According to Catherine, Renita was not respectful to her or her sister, Susan. It was reported that Renita, who recently had turned fifteen, would neither listen nor adhere to house rules, or to instructions at school.

The police had visited the Clays' home on a previous occasion due to some disturbance at a neighbor's house where Renita was attending a class party. The police escorted Renita home because she appeared to have been drinking. Mrs. Clay was told that no record would be made of the visit because Renita was not the reason for them being alerted to the class party, but they cautioned Mrs. Clay to keep an eye on her daughter for her own well-being and safety. Mrs. Clay also wanted to engage in conferencing because of Renita's lack of regard and respect for family members and not keeping her room in a tidy manner.

After brief introductions and during the opening statement, the daughters were reminded that permission from their mother was given to facilitate this conference. While the mother's permission was attained, it was also important for the daughters to give their permission for conferencing. After receiving permission from Renita and Susan to facilitate, they were gently informed of the facilitation process, making them aware of what to expect during the process. Even when a pre-conference is held to give the participants a review of the process, it is still recommended that a brief synopsis of the process be given during the opening statement. After hearing the complete opening statement, and with the understanding that the facilitator would be asking relevant questions regarding issues being discussed, both Susan and Renita offered assurance that they wanted to participate in the dialogue. They even surprised their mother by stating that it was time to have a family meeting because the two of them had some things of their own that both wanted to say.

Ascertaining permission from all parties was indicative of the facilitator's belief that all parties had an interest in seeking a resolution to their concerns and disagreements. Asking the daughters permission to facilitate the conference made them feel part of the discussion. They were informed that even though their mother was present, their opinions were important and should be heard. The opening statement gave them the information they wanted to hear and needed in order for them to participate in honest dialogue. All participants concurred that each party would be able to speak without condemnation and without quick and brash interruptions. The daughters appeared happy about this possibility. Renita made an unexpected announcement of her own. She stated, "I appreciate the facilitator acknowledging me and my sister by asking our permission to ask us questions and not talking to us through our mother. This is the first time I can remember being asked anything. All I can remember hearing, is being told what to do or not to do. Upon arriving here for the conferencing, I had no intentions of participating because I figured we would be traveling a one-way street." As the facilitator, this was a *light-bulb* moment. This acknowledgment from Renita helped set the path for honest and open dialogue.

When the air cleared and discussions commenced, certain hard feelings began being discussed. Mrs. Clay talked about things that would make her happy, such as a civil conversation without the hand palming and respect for family members and house rules. Rinita told how she felt and talked about her defiance for house rules. Renita's disregard for house rules was based on her perception that no one ever listened to her. Susan appeared to be calm and more decisive than her mother and sister. On several occasions, she served as the facilitator for family discussions and was thought as the one who was willing to see and hear both sides. However, Susan had her say. She reminded both her mother and sister how she had witnessed and overheard unkind words spoken between the two, even hearing words about her but not to her. She explained how this sort of communication made her feel excluded and unappreciated, and she wanted it to stop. As the dialogue progressed, miscommunication and the lack of kind words were the root cause for this breakdown in their family harmony.

The conference with Mrs. Clay and her daughters had a pleasant ending. Confessions were made and forgiveness was asked of each other. Written goals and desires were established to remind them of their responsibilities and intentions. The daughters engaged in open dialogue with their mother also. They determined a commonality that was dear to each: Their love for each other along with maintaining peace and harmony in the home.

Bitterness as a result of miscommunication or no communication

When no one is being heard, no one is willing to listen, or even initiate a meaningful discussion, this type of attitude leads to anger, bitterness and indifference. If you are experiencing hurt and disappointment because of how others are perceived to be treating you, pray that God gives you grace to pray for your enemies. There is peace in prayer and contentment in knowing that you hold no grudge against anyone. Unhealthful attitudes can cloud our judgment and negatively alter our behavior if we allow them to linger. There is honor in doing what is best even when it is against our desires. Miscommunication or a misunderstanding gives room for misguided attitudes and behavior. This is why it is important to remember to gather as much factual information as possible before making a harsh judgment. In the best interest of all, look for ways to initiate a discussion on issues that are too important or painful to overlook. It is consistent with biblical principles to seek dialogue with the person you feel has wronged you. "If your brother sins against you, go and show him his fault, just between the two of you. If he listens to you, you have won your brother over" (Matthew 18:15).

Setting the Tone and Atmosphere for Conciliation and Conferencing

The physical environment should be conducive for open and frank dialogue. The room should be uninterrupted, without walk-ins and nonemergency telephone calls. The facilitation site should be physically safe and comfortable with the right room temperature, and such items as water and tissue should be available if needed. The location of the conference should be convenient as possible for all parties.

The facilitator sets the tone of the conferencing by reminding the participants of the elements of the process, such as confidentiality, the opportunity for each participant to be heard without unnecessary or meaningless interruptions, and the willingness to maintain their speech within the bounds of common courtesy.

A comfortable atmosphere helps pave the way for open and honest dialogue where issues and interests can be heard. The effective facilitator recognizes the opportunity to encourage and acknowledge the willingness of the participants to cooperate and commend sincere efforts by the participants to resolve the issues. Genuine validation is welcomed, but an overuse of disingenuous comments can be ineffective. Most participants respond well to a sincere validation but will dismiss meaningless or frivolous remarks, or too many untimely sweet comments used for the purpose of rushing to reach a resolution.

People are different, due sometimes to culture, religion, or national origin, and having the wisdom to accept that difference can lead to open and positive dialogue. Being able to respect each other differences, play a critical part in gaining a meeting of the minds. Empathizing and respecting perceptions of others have a way of softening hostile attitudes and offer the opportunity for a better understanding between the parties.

Homework Assignment

Write a brief summary of this chapter, listing the principles and procedures taught in the text, being as specific as possible.

State how you plan to use some of the principles in your own life when facing a similar situation or other issues.

If you are involved in a group study, consider sharing your summary with other group members for discussion purposes.

Write a letter or prayer thanking God for what you have learned and how certain information has helped you personally.

There is Freedom in Forgiving

CHAPTER NINE

Giving Grace

Facilitation is often viewed as functioning in a leadership capacity. Understanding this normal assumption, an effective facilitator will try to inspire the participants to empower themselves by giving grace through acknowledgment, recognition, and encouragement. As the facilitator is actively engaged in managing the conference, when you notice or perceive that the dialogue is going in a positive direction, and the participants are functioning in a restorative manner by considering the interests of others, be careful to not rush ahead in order to get a quick resolution. Continuing to inspire the participants by acknowledging their progress not only demonstrates effective facilitation skills but is good for the participants to recognize that they are the main characters and what they feel and say are important.

The participants should be the ones to arrive at a viable and mutual resolution because they will be the ones who will live with their own decision. It is more palatable to adhere to a decision that is made by the person who agreed to abide by the agreement.

When facilitating a conference, the facilitator should look for ways to give or provide grace. In this context, giving grace is allowing a participant to save face. There have been times when I have observed an alleged offender demonstrate a hard stance on an issue. Oftentimes the offender has no willingness to reconsider a decision or an action, especially when he or she feels embarrassed to acknowledge any wrong.

I remember a conference where the alleged offender had made an employment termination decision in haste without having all the facts. The alleged issue was about an employee demonstrating insubordination toward a supervisor. The employee explained that the supervisor put his hand on him in an inappropriate and jerking way. The employee, in return, used profanity in telling the supervisor not to personally touch him. The employee's behavior was reported to the operations manager and the employee was sent home without the benefit of a discussion.

During the conference, the employee explained the circumstances surrounding the termination issue. He reported that there were other times when the supervisor had made unwanted or provoked inappropriate advances toward him. At the time the supervisor touched him by jerking on his jacket, the employee admitted that his quick compulsive response might not have been appropriate, but, due to their past working relationship, he wanted to make a strong point to the supervisor to never touch him again.

After continued dialogue by sharing information and getting questions answered by both parties, as the facilitator I asked the operations manager if in hindsight, given what he had heard up to now, would he have made the same decision? Without hesitation, he said, "Hindsight is always better than foresight." At that moment, grace was given to the operations manager to save face. The questions provided the opportunity for the operations manager to acknowledge that to offer the employee an opportunity to discuss the situation first in order to establish a picture from both parties, would perhaps been a fairer and more appropriate way to handle the situation. The dialogue provided the operations manager the opportunity to inform the employee that he had no animosity or dislike for him and that he tried to treat all employees fairly.

As a result of the conference, both parties had a better understanding of each other's position, and both apologized to each other. The employee's termination was reversed, and the relationship between all the parties was improved based upon information that led to the conditions and content of the settlement agreement.

Backing someone into a corner without a way out does not always work well in restorative conferencing. Remaining aware that conferencing is not a trial, rules of evidence do not always apply. Restorative conferencing is about inspiring others to realize what is best rather than focusing on only what is right, and to use their inner strength to make wise and deliberate choices. Even though what is right plays an important role, some decisions are made on what is best served: the better well-being for all parties.

Questions to consider when deciding what is right and what might be best are: "How will my decision impact the outcome of this dispute, and how will my decision impact all concerned parties?" Bear in mind that one might have the *legal* right or given right to consider other options, but will holding someone to the extent of the law or to the letter of the law, accomplish what is sought? The goals are a better relationship, to keep one conscious of his or her actions, and to help all concerned parties experience the joy of receiving and giving grace.

> *"If you forgive men when they sin against you, your heavenly Father will also forgive you" (Matthew 6:14 NIV).*

Freedom in Forgiveness

Why is it important or helpful to forgive? Have you ever decided that you do not want to forgive a certain person for a certain offense, or are you not ready to forgive someone? Biblically speaking, forgiveness is something that you cannot do on your own. Without the Holy Spirit giving you the grace to forgive, you cannot do it alone. With this in mind, you are fighting a losing battle or walking an endless journey by trying to determine when or if you will forgive someone within your own power or will.

How does one forgive another? You can start by asking God for the grace to forgive. You can forgive yourself for your participation or nonparticipation with a given issue. Being able to repent and forgiving yourself help to extend forgiveness to others. Asking for forgiveness from another can be a powerful action in helping to restore a relationship. Offering to forgive, even though you have not been asked, frees you to live a more peaceful life.

How do you know when you have truly forgiven someone?

There are several ways you can know that you have forgiven someone.

> When you think of the person whom you have forgiven, you do not feel anger or vengefulness toward that person.

> You willingly and consciously made a decision to forgive.

> You do not feel a need to think and talk about the person or what was done twenty-four, seven.

> You do not wish harm or revenge upon the offender.

> You are able to continue a relationship with the offender if it is in the best interest of both.

> You can experience the joy and peace of God

Peace in Forgiveness

"A cheerful heart is good medicine, but a crushed spirit dries up the bones" (Proverbs 17:22, The NIV Student Bible).

The real test of forgiveness comes when you are faced with a difficult issue because someone has brought harm or hurt to you. Often we look for ways to justify why we are unable to forgive the person who transgressed against us. We will pontificate the situation by using our own standards for forgiveness, such as the following:

> I will forgive him or her when I get an apology.

> I am not ready to forgive him or her.

> I have a right to be angry.

> I am just trying to let him or her know how I feel.

It is okay if I do not talk with my spouse anymore.

It is all right not to cook for my spouse any more.

It is fine if I stop paying my tithes because of what happened to me at church.

She owes me money, and I am not going to ask her for it.

He started this war, and I am going to finish it.

I will show him who he is dealing with.

"If you, O Lord, kept a record of sins, O Lord, who could stand? But with you there is forgiveness; therefore, you are feared" (Psalm 130:3, The NIV Student Bible).

None of the above self-righteous standards made by a personal will is consistent with God's Word. The following suggestions will help you walk through some of your own thoughts and offer you a different perspective of forgiveness. These are things we should consider when faced with a difficult situation that requires our forgiveness:

Have I ever brought harm or hurt to someone and did not ask for forgiveness?

Did I ever cheat on my taxes without making the necessary correction?

Have I ever taken something not belonging to me without permission?

Have I ever lied to protect or help myself?

Am I keeping a secret of a transgression that I committed, which could possibly hurt someone if revealed?

Have I stopped someone from receiving a blessing just because I did not speak up?

Have I ever kept a possession or ownership of others?

Have I ever intentionally taken a pen, paper, or other items belonging to an organization or employer without permission?

Have I kept silent when someone could have been blessed by my words?

Why did I not tell my boss about my friend who qualified for a job opening?

Have I always confessed my sins and asked for forgiveness?

Should I forgive my husband or friend for his or her transgression, so I can have peace with myself and God?

Have I willfully withheld information that could have helped someone else?

Has God forgiven me for my transgressions?

Have I ever been given a second chance?

God's Word is very clear on how and why we should forgive. Forgiveness is for the wounded. Once you have, through God's grace, forgiven the offender, it not only releases you form bondage of another, it brings you freedom, joy, and peace with self and with God.

"Then Peter came to Jesus and asked, 'Lord, how many times shall I forgive my brother when he sins against me up to seven times?' Jesus answered, 'I tell you, not seven times, but seventy-seven times.'" Matthew, 18:21-22. It is clear that there is no limit on the number of times you must forgive another; it is only by God's grace that we are even able to forgive the first time. We, as human beings, are not capable of forgiving anyone on our own. The world's view is far different for God's view. One might say, "Kick 'em to the curb" or "feed them with a long-handled spoon", or even "Don't get angry, get even."; "God is a spirit, and his worshipers must worship in spirit and in truth" (John 4:24, the NIV Student Bible).

"What causes fights and quarrels among you? Don't they come from your desires that battle within you?"(James, 4:1, the NIV Student Bible). Unbridled thoughts can lead to stress, depression, and other unhealthy conditions. It is necessary to check our thoughts and line them up with biblical principles.

Homework Assignment

Write a brief summary of this chapter, listing the principles and procedures taught in the text, being as specific as possible.

State how you plan to use some of the principles in your own life when facing a similar situation or other issues.

If you are involved in a group study, consider sharing your summary with other group members for discussion purposes.

Write a letter or prayer thanking God for what you have learned and how certain information has personally helped you.

"Brothers if anyone is caught in a sin, you who are spiritual should restore him gently. But watch yourself, or you also may be tempted" (Galatians 6:1 NIV).

CHAPTER TEN

Helping Harm's Way

Some participants in this scenario were the result of getting involved as good Samaritans using unwise diplomacy. The story I am sharing is altered to protect the identities of the participants. On an early Monday morning starting about two o'clock in the morning, several young people had attended a concert, some went home and went to bed and others went home and continued the party, even inviting others over to just have a good time. Drinking alcohol and using controlled substances were part of this party. The yard light was on and people were in the yard since this was a warm summer morning. As people walked by, some stopped to join the conversation on the porch. One particular gentleman started to get a little riotous and loud with a friend. Next, two young gentlemen with the hearts of Samaritans heard the ruckus and decided they would check out the situation while feeling invincible under the influence of drugs and alcohol.

After they approached the home and inquired about the loud noise—a male companion talking loudly to another friend—they were politely asked to dismiss themselves from the premises. Al and Tim, the Samaritans, made the judgment to inform the gentleman who was loud-talking his friend that this type of conduct was not appropriate and he should cease from using certain language. The good Samaritans were again reminded to leave, and they refused. A physical struggle began after the loud-talking gentleman stepped toward Tim and he thought someone touched or pushed him. Tim and two other party participants were hurt because a group of four or five people started fighting each other without actually knowing the facts. How the fight was started no one knew for sure. Police were called and a report was taken by the police from those who were fighting. As a result of being one of the facilitators who had the privilege of conferencing with the participants, we talked about ways to avoid confrontations, especially when it is possible to do so.

The following is a list of values that were determined one could use to minimize confrontations and conflict, as well as legal and financial consequences:

Pause and Think

Pause, take a deep breath and walk away.

Think of the consequences of your actions.

Consider the impact your actions will have on others (family members, friends, and community).

Count the cost of a legal trial and medical cost.

Consider the time spent to heal the harm.

Consider what it is like to spend some time in jail.

Consider your reputation.

What impact will this offense have on your life now and in the future?

Could this action subsequently become a felony on my record?

Could this violation stop me from getting a job later in life?

Is it possible that I could incur or cause someone else to incur bodily harm?

Is it worth your effort?

If you do not have time to pause and think, just call the police and allow them to do their job when others are in violation of the law.

Homework Assignment

Write a brief summary of this chapter, listing the principles and procedures taught in the text, being as specific as possible.

State how you plan to use some of the principles in your own life when facing a similar situation or other issues.

If you are involved in a group study, consider sharing your summary with other group members for discussion purposes.

Write a letter or prayer thanking God for what you have learned and how certain information has personally helped you.

"Trust in the Lord with all your heart and lean not on your own understanding; in all your ways acknowledge him, and he will make your paths straight" (Proverbs 3:5-6 NIV).

CHAPTER 11

Deciding a Decision

In an e-mail received from a parent whose daughter had graduated from high school, the mother was asking me to call her daughter and encourage her in her aspirations of going to college and establishing new friendships. Being somewhat familiar with the daughter's behavior through personal conversations with the daughter and mother, it gave me a sense of direction on how to word statements and suggestions during our conversation. Generally it helps the facilitator to engage in effective dialogue or writing when encouraging someone you know a little about.

Emily, the daughter, possessed a straightforward attitude and a strong will. Her demeanor would not indicate or lead one to believe that, just because something was said, she would readily accept and apply this information to her situation. This statement in no way suggests that Emily is a self-proclaimed know-it-all. Quite the opposite. Emily is a very smart and bright young person graduating with honors and would be attending a major university on a scholarship. She thoughtfully and methodically analyzed her choices before making a decision. On occasion, she had even sought my opinion on personal issues in her life.

Considering all that I know about Emily, I constructed a list of options for her to evaluate to determine if any would be useful for her. As you read through these options and concerns, carefully analyze each and determine which ones you might be able to use in your own life experiences and temptations.

What Is a Decision-Making Process?

A sound and structured thought process is essential in making an enlightened decision. When structuring your thought process, be aware of your own characteristics. In other words, be true to yourself. Knowing who you are and what you are able and most likely to live with should help guide you through a process of making the best decision. If you know that something is certain to challenge your core values, or you could not bear to live with the consequences, that should be considered a red flag for you to give careful thought and consideration before making a definite decision to do or not to do something. When something could be of a potentially criminal consequence, a negative response seems to be a wise decision. If you can determine that the consequences or potential consequences of a certain action or behavior are too severe for you to cope or live with, do not commit the action.

A Structured Process for Decision-Making

> Consider who you are as a person and how this decision will impact your life in a short time, a long time, or for life.
>
> Consider how a decision will impact others, family, children friends, church, or community.
>
> When given a deadline to make a decision, first determine if meeting that deadline is sufficient time for you to be comfortable in making that decision.
>
> You have the power to say yes, no, or delay a decision.
>
> Think of hypothetical situations that you might expect to come into your life, and then, after careful consideration and

evaluation, decide how you would generally determine your decision on how you would respond.

Determining your decision as much as possible before an event or circumstance happens in your life, gives you time to reconsider a decision. Since we cannot exactly create an event that has not happened with definite precision, having rehashed a similar scenario will jog your memory to think about the best way to handle a certain situation. It is also helpful to think about how you can just say *no* in the event you are faced with a situation that requires it as the best answer.

Remember to be empathetic with others when it is beneficial to do so. Sincere empathy can help others understand why you might say *no* to a given issue.

Know what you can be definite about, such as in what situations I will give a definite no, yes, or maybe.

Consider if your decision will cause harm to yourself or others.

Will you and others benefit by a particular decision or commitment?

Is your decision consistent with Godly principles?

Homework Assignment

Write a brief summary of this chapter, listing the principles and procedures taught in the text, being as specific as possible.

State how you plan to use some of the principles in your own life when facing a similar situation or other issues.

If you are involved in a group study, consider sharing your summary with other group members for discussion purposes.

Write a letter or prayer thanking God for what you have learned and how certain information has personally helped you.

"And the son said to him, 'Father, I have sinned against heaven and in your sight; I am no longer worthy to be called your son.' But the father said to his slaves, Quickly bring out the best robe and put it on him, and put a ring on his hand and sandals on his feet; and bring the fattened calf, kill it, and let us eat and be merry; for this son of mine was dead, and has come to life again; he was lost, and has been found. And they began to be merry," (Luke, 15:21-24 NAST).

CHAPTER TWELVE

The Absentee Father Scenario

Susie is nearing the season in her life of becoming a senior citizen. She has worked faithfully and diligently to maintain a caring home life for her three children and herself. Susie managed going back to school while working long hours on her job to sustain her family and received her undergraduate degree. Being married early in her life, Susie felt that she had met her soul mate and the spouse of her dream. Rob was a handsome and fun guy to be with. Even though not always employed, he showed promise and potential. Initially Rob and Susie shared a happy home life with their children: Tonya, Troy, and Terry. All three did very well in high school and college, maintaining good grades and managing to stay away from trouble. Tonya even received a rare scholarship that carried her through her undergraduate and graduate degrees. After graduating from college, Troy and Terry were fortunate to find great jobs in their respective areas.

During the early years of Rob and Susie's marriage, something went wrong. Rob's employment became more and more dismal. More times off from employment than being employed was the norm for him. Financial woes plagued the marriage resulting in separations and getting back together, which happened several times. A divorce was finally granted after years of shuffling through motions of reconciliation without attaining a satisfactory remedy. During the times of separations, Rob was absent from the home. Susie tried to explain the absenteeism to her children without the hurt and pain she inherited. Susie never spoke negatively of Rob with her children. Tonya, being the eldest, was impacted more than her younger brothers because she felt that more responsibility was placed upon her and she had to be strong for her mother and siblings. She felt anger and bitterness toward her father and oftentimes did not make her emotions known by keeping her feelings silent. Tonya was careful not to bother her mother about anything that might bring her some degree of anxiety and was very protective of her. She often encouraged Terry and Troy to be kind and helpful to their mom. She helped them in keeping their room tidy.

After the three siblings graduated from college, they moved from their family home and started new lives with new friendships of their own. Susie continued to work and purchased rental property to enhance her income. Going to work, taking care of chores, paying bills, enjoying the fruit of their labor, they all were living convenient and comfortable lives. After many uneventful years, they received news that Rob had passed. Even though their relationship with Rob's parents remained strong, Rob's whereabouts were not always known. During the early years of high school and college, Troy and Terry also experienced some anger and bitterness due to their father's absence in their lives. They wanted their father available to share what was happening in their lives and to seek his advice. They talked often between themselves and often wondered how nice it would be if Rob were there because there were things they did not want to share with Susie. They wanted Rob to be there for them. Susie never totally gave up on Rob—she was acutely aware that Rob loved his children—but just did not demonstrate the capacity of being able to sustain a relationship during his absence. There was virtually no communication with Rob during the several times of separations. Rob's parents were faithful in helping Susie with the needs of the children: buying clothes, sending gifts, and even giving financially to Susie to help with books, food, and school activities.

Upon learning that Rob had passed, all three siblings talked among themselves and decided that they did not want to attend their father's funeral. Susie was desperate for them to attend the funeral not just to respect the passing of their father, but she felt Rob's parents would be pleased to see their grandchildren at the funeral. Rob was an only child and was loved dearly by his parents. His death was devastating to his parents. Their whole life had revolved around Rob since he was born. They were his safety net during the times of unemployment. I received a visit from Susie seeking help in trying to arrive at a positive response and resolution for all concerned. After a long one-on-one conference with Susie, she decided that she would share the details discussed during our conferencing with her daughter and two sons. Several days after our discussion, Susie informed me that all three siblings attended the funeral, and the grandparents were very happy to see them.

Essence of the Conferencing Details

Releasing as a form of forgiveness

An unforgiving heart could be viewed as a form of control. This type of control is present while trying to control a living human being, but when it is used to try to control the dead you are no longer controlling anyone; moreover, the situation is now controlling you. Rob's spirit was not with his body any longer. The land of the living no longer matters nor is part of Rob's immortality. He can no longer be impacted by the actions of others. Limiting another's capacity to participate in grieving another's death, especially a family member, by not attending a funeral or participating in celebrations, is a form of controlling. Trying to impact the dead by any means for any practical purpose is useless. When a debt is released or forgiven, it is no longer owed or held against a person or entity. An unforgiving spirit is not consistent with biblical principles. "For if you forgive men for their transgressions, your heavenly Father will also forgive you. But, if you do not forgive men, then your Father will not forgive your transgressions" (Matthew 6:14 and 15, NAST).

What is right vs. what is best?

When given a situation that you want to control, try determining what is right and what is best for a resolution. Taking into consideration Rob's absence and nonparticipation during most of his children's lives, it is easy to say that the children had a right not to attend Rob's funeral if this were their desire. However, considering Susie's desire to attend the funeral and for the children to attend, and remembering the kindness, support, and love of Rob's parents, is it now easier to arrive at the right resolution or the best resolution? Honoring the best decision brings peace, comfort, and oftentimes happiness not only to oneself but also to others who are affected. Initially the best resolution might not be according to your will, but, knowing that it was made for a better and higher cause than for yourself, peace and harmony will be rewarding results.

Controlling by omission or elimination

This type of controlling is often demonstrated in organizations or group orientations. For example, when a leader or one who is in an authoritative position has an unforgiving heart and uses this power to eliminate, limit, or exclude the talent of another person because of a personal dislike, this becomes a form of controlling. Overlooking, omitting, or eliminating the use of someone's ability that could benefit others, are all cowardly acts of controlling. The victim of such behavior is not the only one who is impacted. Others who are part of the group, work environment, or organization are denied the benefit of the victim's useful services.

It is helpful for us to recognize the difference between facts and perceptions. Knowing the difference offers a better insight into making appropriate decisions. "Each of you should look not only to your own interests, but also to the interest of others" (Philippians 2:4, NAST), and "Do not be overcome by evil, but overcome evil with good" (Romans 12:21). "A man's wisdom gives him patience, it is to his glory to overlook an offense" (Proverbs 19:11, (NIV). When you are unable to release another person from a long-held, painful perception, it is like throwing out a treasure because it is not wrapped in a gift box. Peace is a reward of forgiveness. Peace is an intangible gift that displays itself in healthful ways. Respect, love, a helping hand, and other sources of good deeds do not always come in beautifully wrapped packages. God's love is invisible but is manifested physically, spiritually, and emotionally.

Homework Assignment

Write a brief summary of this chapter, listing the principles as taught in the text, being as specific as possible

State how you plan to use some of the principles in your own life when facing a similar situation or other issues.

If you are involved in a group study, consider sharing your summary with other group members for discussion purposes.

Write a letter or prayer thanking God for what you have learned and how certain information has personally helped you.

"The mind of sinful man is death, but the mind controlled by the Spirit is life and peace" (Romans, 8:6 NIV).

CHAPTER THIRTEEN

Allowing the Dead to Control the Living

Perceptions or Facts

There are times when perceptions become cloudy and the holder becomes convinced that what he or she is thinking is a reality. Consider when the desires of the deceased are carried out according to the terms of a will or a living trust. Since a will or trust is made while one is living, the terms are not activated until after death; therefore, to some degree, the desires of the deceased can prevail if not contested or modified by the courts.

James Whittaker had accumulated a mass of wealth by becoming a successful businessperson. James initially started an Internet-based business from the basement of his home and he had two employees: his wife Sybil and himself. They worked diligently to grow the company by creating a great website. The business thrived by using innovative avenues and networks on the web. Over a span of a decade, the business grew to a billion-dollar enterprise with more than five hundred employees. James and his wife had an only daughter, Jamie, who graduated from a local university with honors, receiving her graduate degree. Needless to say, her parents were very proud and had high expectations for her. Soon after Jamie received her degree, her mother died from a rare illness. It was now just James and Jamie, who was the apple of his eye.

Without being officially engaged, Jamie decided to marry her high school sweetheart, Peter, who James never considered a suitable catch. James made very attractive business offers to Jamie if she considered postponing her marriage to Peter and continued working for the family business. He even offered her a partnership in the business, which came earlier than he had planned. James wanted Jamie to earn her way in the business in order to maintain respect from other employees. James and Sybil had provided all of Jamie's needs until she started working in the family business. James wanted Jamie to be an independent person not expecting to be given everything on a silver platter.

Unknown to Jamie, James had his eye on one of his young, bright vice presidents for a son-in-law. James was introduced to Ethan at a prototype exhibit where certain inventions were judged and hopefully found sponsors. Before joining James's company, Ethan had his own invention at an exhibit when he caught the attention of James Whittaker. Ethan created an office gadget that could process and help track the value of an employee's work in the company. After meeting and talking with Ethan for some time, James invited him to visit his office, where James offered Ethan a job.

Before Jamie announced to her father her engagement to Peter, James made sure that she got the chance to meet Ethan. Since the company had grown so large, it could not be taken for granted that everybody knew each other. James arranged an employee party and instructed that Ethan and Jamie work on the party's planning committee along with other selected employees. Peter was anxious and happy to marry Jamie. They were not officially engaged but had talked about marriage and children. Peter was a struggling musician who was working local gigs and looking for a big break by being noticed at one of his assignments. Peter did not have a regular job, and James thought he was just lazy. Mr. Whittaker decided privately that if Jamie insisted on getting married to Peter, he would have his attorney construct a will or a living trust that stipulated how his wealth would be used and distributed after his death.

James's opinion was that if he just bequeathed everything to his daughter, Peter would have full benefit and access to her inheritance. He was convinced that Jamie would give Peter anything he wanted, including financing his entertainment dreams. After James sought the advice of his attorney and financial advisor, a very sophisticated trust was constructed. James stipulated how Jamie could make withdrawals from the trust and at what times the withdrawals could be made. He even stipulated that Jamie had to make a written, itemized request in order to receive her funds. Her request must be consistent with the purpose as stated in the trust. In no way was Jamie to make any request for funds on behalf of Peter. Jamie could only withdraw up to a certain amount each year. Provisions for the grandchildren, if there were any, were also arranged. The grandchildren would receive a lump sum upon graduating for college. All educational expenses were to be paid from the trust. Other conditions regarding grandchildren working for the company, and how they should be rewarded beyond their earned salaries, were also made part of the trust.

James stated that he wanted to be able to control his wealth after his death, even if it meant controlling some aspects of his daughter's life. He mentioned that he wanted to be as certain as possible that the labor of his hand would be respected by his descendants.

After James's death, Jamie and Peter's relationship was short lived, not because of Mr. Whittaker's desires or any terms of his trust, Jamie decided that their compatibility and Peter's commitment in the relationship were not strong enough to survive a marriage. Jamie had no problem with adhering to the terms of her father's trust.

Releasing the Dead

<u>A War between the Dead and the Living</u>

A church that I once attended offered many ministries and community outreach programs and provided much support for its missions. Aside from a myriad of educational programs and an elementary church school, a noted Bible Institute for advanced learning was established. I consider myself fortunate being able to take advantage of its Bible seminars.

A cherished memory was when I enrolled in a Bible counseling course that was taught by a psychologist along with a couple of professional counselors from the church.

During this training, the curriculum allowed for student roll play. The roll playing groups consisted of three people: the facilitator, counselee, and a critiquing observer. Each participant participated in each of the three rolls. Before starting the roll play, we all introduced ourselves and shared our particular backgrounds. Being a practicing mediator, I was somewhat familiar with the probing aspect of facilitating. We were instructed to follow the counseling format that was taught in class.

As we followed the instructions set out by the course facilitators, including the introductions, other preliminaries, and a few pleasantries, Mark began to tell his story. His mother passed at birth and he was raised by his father. Mark, the counselee, shared that, in his opinion, he could never do enough for his father. He felt that he was never good enough and he would always look for his father's approval. Mark's greatest desire was to get approval from his father. During the probing aspect of the session, we learned that his father was very strict and raised him with military discipline. Mark talked about how hard he worked to please his father by studying long hours, making good grades, and helping around the house, but still he never heard the words, "Son, I am proud of you," or "I love you" from his father.

Mark was also asked how he felt about himself and his accomplishments. He quickly stated that he was very proud of his accomplishments, which included completing college with two degrees, and working for the state where he earned a decent salary. During the roll play, we learned that Mark was seeing a psychiatrist on a regular basis, working toward healing his depression. Mark still was trying to please his father. To our surprise, when Mark was asked if he was in regular contact with his father at the present time, he quietly stated that his father passed away two years ago. Through more probing, we tried to learn if Mark, in his opinion, knew exactly what his father wanted from him. He responded by saying, "No, I could never really understand what he wanted me to do, or what I could do on my own to please him." According to Mark, his father was not a very verbal person, especially when it came to complimenting someone or showing any admiration with emotions. His father was neither emotional nor too wordy when expressing himself.

We discovered a lot during our exploratory session. The facilitator encouraged Mark, asked if he were comfortable telling us a little more about his father. We were informed that Mark's father paid for all of his educational expense; paid for his clothing, and made sure his son's needs were met medically, financially, and physically. Mark's father worked very hard and provided him with a comfortable home and other nice things that Mark wanted. We further noticed that his father was not abusive in any way. He would carry Mark to church with him while he was a child at home. We asked Mark if he ever felt that he could ask his father if he was proud of him. Mark never thought that he could ask his father if he were proud of him as a person; he explained that he preferred his father telling him that directly. Other open-ended questions were explored with Mark. For example, we asked, "How do you feel about your father in other ways as a parent? Was he kind and available to you? Were you allowed to have friends visit when you were younger?

Mark began to rethink the relationship he shared with his father. He said, "You know, I have been so depressed until I had forgotten the good things my father did for me. I have been depressed to the point of staying in bed all day, and I have even gone days, even a month, without bathing." Mark shared that his father, other than being virtually nonverbal, was a good and kind person. They played ball together when he was younger, and his father would take him to the zoo when time permitted. His father worked long hours when Mark was younger, to the point of having to hire a nanny. Mark remembers his first suit his father purchased for him—it was his fifteenth birthday. Tears began to well up in his eyes. He said, "I just wanted my dad to tell me that he loved me and was proud of me. I guess he showed that in a different way by doing the best he knew how."

Mark stated that, "My father had seven siblings and my grandfather worked very hard and was rarely at home for family conversations. Yet he would tell me about my granddad, how generous he was and how happy the family would be, especially on Sundays when my granddad was home and did not have to work."

Mark wanted us to know that, during our session, he was able to realize that his father had his own way of showing his approval of him. He even bought Mark a new car when he was ready to attend college. After the roll play, Mark stated that he could now release his father and forgive himself and his father for holding such painful perceptions. Mark said right in our small group, "I am free. I can now cherish the true and good memories of my father." Mark declared he would no longer be controlled by a grave by giving his power to the dead. He further shared that he regretted not being able to see through his own selfish perceptions. Before we left our group meeting, Mark indicated that he would share what happened in our roll play with his psychiatrist. Restorative conferencing plays a crucial role in inspiring people to look at a situation from more than one perspective. It helps us to see others from a more realistic and less selfish point of view.

After some time passed and a new semester began, I passed Mark in the hallway one day. We greeted each other and Mark responded, "I am on my own. I am not seeing my psychiatrist at the present time." Being open and honest with others whom you trust enable you to analyze your own perceptions and inner strengths. By doing so, you are able to see more clearly from the viewpoint of others and see things differently through your own insight.

Homework Assignment

Write a brief summary of this chapter, listing the principles taught in the text, being as specific as possible.

State how you plan to use some of the principles in your own life when facing a similar situation or other issues.

If you are involved in a group study, consider sharing your summary with other group members for discussion purposes.

Write a letter or prayer thanking God for what you have learned and how certain information has personally helped you.

BUILDING EFFECTIVE LISTENING SKILLS

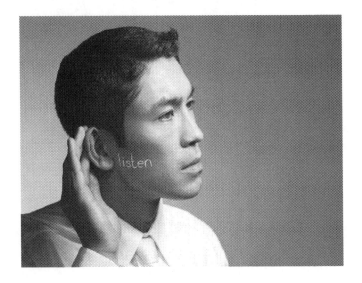

CHAPTER FOURTEEN

Building Effective Listening Skills

Effective listening skills are crucial to gaining a clear understanding of what the issues are about. When facilitating a group discussion, whether it is for conferencing, or any other group activity, exercising good communication skills provide benefits. It assures the participants that they are being heard, and it provides the facilitator with an in-depth insight of the dispute. Listening skills entail understanding what another person is saying by paraphrasing what was said. Effective listening skills demonstrate the facilitator's sincerity in being genuinely interested in hearing another's point of view. People want to know that they are being heard especially when involved in a conflict. Disputes and disagreements are the reason for coming to the table to discuss issues in a more structured manner because someone feels like he or she has not been heard.

Practicing the following suggested skills will enhance your listening skills to a sufficient level to acquire a comprehensive view of the dispute.

Paraphrasing

According to various dictionaries, "Paraphrasing is a restatement of dialogue or text using other words. A paraphrase typically explains or clarifies the text that is being paraphrased. For example, *'The signal was red'* might be paraphrased as *the train was not allowed to proceed.* When accompanying the original statement, a paraphrase is usually introduced with a declaratory expression to signal the transition to the paraphrase. For example, in the *signal was red, that is, the train was not allowed* to proceed, 'the *"that is",* signals the paraphrase that follows. Paraphrasing aims to retain the intent of the message that is being rephrased."

References: James H. Morey, "Peter Comestor, Biblical Paraphrase, and the Medieval Popular Bible," Speculum, vol.68, no. 1, Jan. 1993, pp. 6-35, and http://en.wikipedia.org/wiki/Parapharase.

Carefully paraphrasing can bring about a better understanding of what was said. For example, an offender might say, "I took his coat because it was raining." When paraphrasing, the facilitator could say, "Are you saying you do not own a coat?" Using the restorative approach to resolve conflict creates better results when choosing the best words for a given situation. A careful use of voice tone or words is useful in calming tempers and decreasing the chance of sounding accusatory or too blunt. Thus, allowing a question to lead into paraphrasing is like asking permission to hold a certain understanding of what was said and gives grace to the maker of the statement.

Reframing

One definition of reframing is when someone makes a statement, and that statement is altered by interjecting other options or considerations in order to achieve a particular goal or mutual satisfaction. For example, someone makes the statement, "I would like to bring my daughter to the party, but I do not have a car." Someone else says, "If someone could come and pick you and your daughter up and carry you back home, would your daughter be able to come to the party?"

Reframing is altering a phrase by changing the words and putting it into a context that is consistent with the intent of the altered phrase. One could easily assert that, in essence, when someone is telling his or her story, and certain phrases are extrapolated from the story and restated but still makes a mirrored version of what was spoken is considered reframing.

Clarifying

Clarifying can be as simple as repeating what was said and adding a more descriptive version of the statement in order to get a better understanding. Two people are in a disagreement about one being late for a business meeting. The chairman accused a committee member of being late. The respondent stated that she was on time, but when she got to the committee room she knocked at the door and no one answered. To clarify this statement, a question could be asked: "Are you saying you were here *on time* and you could not come in because the door to the committee room was locked?" This question calls for a better understanding than, "No one answered my knock at the door."

Benefits of Effective Listening Skills

- It assures the speaker that he or she is being heard, and a better understanding of what was said is given.
- It demonstrates sincerity about learning the facts of the situation.
- It could help to validate the speaker's point of view regarding the issues being discussed.
- It gives the listeners a fair assessment of the issues being discussed.
- It helps the participants feel like they are being heard and promotes respect and empathy within the context of the issues.

Controlling and Listening to Your Own Silent Thoughts

Each of us has silent thoughts and conversations just with ourselves. Our thoughts are very important, regardless how profound or insignificant they might be. For the baker, one creates new recipes by silently thinking about what ingredients should go into a particular dish. Then the cook will put his or her silent thoughts into action by mixing, stirring, and baking. If the dish is tasty, a new dish is created and receives a name given by its owner.

Teachers silently think about what questions will be on a given examination. They consider the objectives covered in the class and what has been taught. From this point, an examination is constructed to determine the students' level of knowledge based on given assignments and what was taught in class. Some thoughts are good and helpful while others might be destructive and not useful. It is our thoughts that guide our path of actions when implemented. This is why careful thought should be given to evaluating them. Consider if a particular thought is implemented, and how this action would impact your personal life for now, one month from now, a year from now, ten years from now, or for life. Some actions can have immediate consequences or nine months from now depending on the nature of the action. Take time to ask how this action would create disharmony in the lives of others such as family, church, friends, and community members; ask how my actions might bring harm to myself or others. Someone might ask, "How can my personal acts affect my community?" When crime runs rampantly in a given community, property values can be affected. A home is often the largest investment some people would ever make. Having their property devalued due to the selfish actions of others brings unwanted consequences, and it causes financial harm.

<u>Controlling your silent thoughts</u>

Deciding a decision for actions must be given careful and critical examination. Before a principle or law is violated, serious thought must be given to a decision. Often when a decision is made to act upon a vile or lawless thought, the person holding that thought does not always consider the consequences; therefore when a lawless act is committed, and when time is given to reconsider the actions, the offender regrets his participation because of the consequences. Once a thought is acted upon, it is no longer a thought. It is a reality. When there is doubt about taking an action, do not take the action if dire consequences can be the results.

Thoughts or ideas

Thoughts are often just passing memories without giving further consideration. When thoughts are allowed to linger and you ponder whether this can become a reality, it is now an idea. Unbridled thoughts and ideas can lead to multiple mistakes and offenses. Being prepared to eject unhealthy thoughts from our minds and redirect our thoughts to a more constructive path will enable us to live more productive lives that will guard us from potential harm.

Take time to evaluate negative ideas. If an idea directs you to commit a crime or cause harm to yourself or others, do not entertain such idea. Do not even discuss it with potential partners in crime. Control negative ideas before carrying them out. For example, if you are feeling desperate enough to commit a crime, take time to consider the consequences. Consider other alternatives that will bring better results. If you must have money, reject robbing another person or bank. Think of ways you might enable yourself to earn an income. Consider a trade or seek help provided by local agencies to assist you in times of emergencies. One principle to remember is this: *If you do not want to suffer the consequences, do not commit the crime.*

"Finally, brethren, whatever is true, whatever is honorable, whatever is right, whatever, is pure, whatever is lovely, whatever is of good repute, if there is any excellence and if anything worthy of praise, let your mind dwell on these things" (Philippians 4:8, NAST).

Importance of controlling your thoughts

A one-on-one conversation with a young man (whom we will call Lance) revealed the trouble he had sleeping after retiring for the night and getting into bed. After a very busy day and working hours extending far beyond an eight-hour day, he looked forward to coming home, relaxing and talking with the family. Lance would stay up late at night preparing for his first task the next morning at work or until he became too sleepy to concentrate on anything.

Lance shared that, as soon as he had gotten into bed, he would not be very sleepy. His mind was filled with thoughts of the current day, but his thoughts would only remain for just a short span of time. He would start thinking about something very different or something that had happed in the distant past. Lance talked about when he tried to pray, his prayers would be interrupted by wandering thoughts. He told how annoying it was when he was not in control of his own thoughts. He described his sleep as short and tiresome naps. In the morning, rather than feeling fresh and ready to start the day, he was feeling tired and irritable.

We talked about the possibility of him seeking medical help. He confided that he was already taking prescription medication to help him sleep, but he would only take the medication when the night was passing him by without sleeping, and he felt the need to get some degree of sleep before starting the next day. Lance preferred not taking medication unless it was an absolute necessity. Lance believed that if he could control his silent thoughts, sometimes healthy and at times not so healthy; he could sleep without medication. He worried about his job and what happens on his job. As a Christian, Lance felt he should be able to at least control how he prayed, but even then these unwanted thoughts penetrated his mind; and before he could finish praying, his thoughts had wandered off to other places or issues. Some were so insignificant, such as *Perhaps I should try using that new soap bar, I received for a present, to shower with in the morning, or which will be the best restaurant to have a business lunch with an important client?"*

Lance's silent, interrupting thoughts had begun to irritate him because he took great pride in being in control of certain job responsibilities and just being able to be "on top of things," as he put it. Something as simple as not being able to sleep because of wandering and nagging thoughts did not sit well with him. Since Lance relied on God's Word for guidance, we decided to search the Scriptures in order to find a remedy for his sleepless nights. He first eliminated a medical reason for his sleeplessness. His doctor had informed him that he did not have sleep apnea. Since there was not a medical problem to deal with, Lance felt that he should be able, to some degree, to control his own thoughts.

First, we decided that it would be helpful to Lance by just asking for divine grace to help him in controlling his thoughts. According to Scripture, we should trust God in all of our ways, because with God all things are possible. "Trust in the Lord with all your heart, and do not lean on your own understanding. In all your ways acknowledge Him, and He will make your paths straight" (Proverbs, 3:5–6).

We can train our minds to think of good things. When bad thoughts start penetrating our mind as nagging thoughts, ask for grace to control those thoughts. It is not possible to rid ourselves of thoughts, otherwise that might call for the brain to be examined, but what we can do is to control our thoughts and redirect them to more constructive and healthier matters. We are judged by our actions rather than thoughts. No one knows for certain what another person's thoughts are; being able to control our own thoughts, thereby controlling our actions, helps us to grow morally and mentally.

Remembering and recalling certain Scripture relevant to certain issues can help keep us focused on doing what is appropriate. According to Isaiah, 26:3, "You will keep him in perfect peace, whose mind is stayed on You, because he trusts in You" (Gideons Bible). Scripture reminds us of the importance of a renewed mind.

After engaging in an insightful conference with Lance, we discovered that his mind was overloaded with life-challenging situations. He spent most of his day thinking of other things rather than on what was at hand at the time. He was working on a new assignment at work and did not feel comfortable with his level of expertise for this particular job. While working on a job project, he was thinking about how he could improve his job skills, how could he get out of a few debts, and how long he would be able to make the mortgage payments on his home if he were ever unemployed.

The thoughts that occupied Lance's mind were now practically controlling his mind; he was in desperate need to alter his thought pattern. We discussed Romans; 12:2 (NIV) "Do not conform any longer to the pattern of this world, but be transformed by the renewing of your mind. Then you will be able to test and approve what God's will is—his good, pleasing and perfect will." Lance and I discussed ways of redirecting his thoughts by focusing on things that were pleasant and spending more time thinking of things in the moment. After our conferencing session, Lance decided to take control of his thoughts rather than having his thoughts control him. From Scripture we learn that, "For the mind set on the flesh is death, but the mind set on the Spirit is life and peace, because the mind set on the flesh is hostile toward God; for it does not subject itself to the law of God, for it is not even able to do so," Romans, 8:6 NAST.

After certain options were explored and considered, this is what Lance decided to try:

He would seek divine guidance and grace in redirecting his thought pattern.

He would de-clutter his mind by replacing negative and nagging thoughts with more healthful thoughts.

He would stay focused on what he was doing at the moment and not allow his mind to wander.

He would seek help on a new job assignment when he was not confident with his skill level. However, he did not want his manager to think that he could not handle the job because it was within the scope of his training. Lance decided to approach a trusted coworker, who had performed the job that was now his responsibility, for help.

He would spend time in devising a personal budget that was within his means.

If necessary, he would seek credit counseling.

Lance stated that he would start ejecting negative, nonproductive thoughts as soon as they entered his mind and would replace them with more helpful things with a sense of direction.

The Scripture teaches, "Finally, brothers, whatever is true, whatever is noble, whatever is right, whatever is pure, whatever is lovely, whatever is admirable—if anything is excellent or praiseworthy—think about such things" (Philippians 4:8 NIV).

"We demolish arguments and every pretension that sets itself up against the knowledge of God, and we take captive every thought to make it obedient to Christ," (2nd Corinthians, 10:5 NIV).

Homework Assignment

Write a brief summary of this chapter, listing the principles and techniques taught in the text, being as specific as possible.

State how you plan to use some of the principles in your own life when facing a similar situation or other issues.

If you are involved in a group study, consider sharing your summary with other group members for discussion purposes.

Write a letter or prayer thanking God for what you have learned and how certain information has personally helped you.

"Precious in the sight of the Lord is the death of his saints" (Psalm 116:15 NIV).

CHAPTER FIFTEEN

Conferencing the Bereaved

When conferencing with a bereaved family or person, be cautious not to be make premature judgments about how a person should or should not grieve. People are different with personal emotions. More than likely, the deceased had a special and different relationship with the people he or she knew; therefore careful consideration should be given to each person's emotions with respect to the type of relationship shared with the deceased.

A child grieving the death of a parent would have different emotions grieving the death of a sibling. Depending on the age of the child, emotions could be based on the need in the relationship. If a deceased sibling was the caretaker of a child, the emotions would be similar to grieving a parent. A person's emotions would be different when connected to the death of a friend than with a spouse. Emotions can vary depending upon the relationship with the deceased.

No immediate time limit should be placed upon grieving; however, if grieving escalates to severe depression or manifests itself in a more dire or severe manner, seeking professional or medical attention would be in order. After talking with many clients, I discovered that some people enjoy remembering and talking about certain characteristics of the deceased. The grieving process is often based on the type of relationship held with the deceased. After one is able to accept the death of a loved one, sweet memories still linger. One lady shared with me how she enjoyed talking about her husband and remembering the happy and wonderful times they shared together. Three months after her husband's passing, she was still carrying in her purse a copy of his obituary. To some, this might seem odd, but, for this wonderful lady, it was her way of coping with the loss of her husband.

Recognizing when conferencing has reached its limits demonstrates that you, as the facilitator, have been listening and hearing the bereaved. While conferencing with a certain client, she explained that she was receiving too many visitors and telephone calls from friends and family, given a lot of advice and too many instructions. Even though the support was well intended, my client felt that she was exhausted from having so much attention. While this might be acceptable with some people who are grieving, it could be a little overwhelming for others. Sandra, the name for this client, contended that she needed some time alone to reflect on her life before losing her loved one, and time to just be alone with her private thoughts. This could be exactly what was needed; if signs of severe depression are expressed or demonstrated directly or indirectly by hinting or casually mentioning something that might appear to be irregular or abnormal, do not be too shy to ask about getting medical or appropriate professional help that the situation might require.

Remain aware that genuine concern and care are to be cherished and need to be treated with much sensitivity. If the bereaved is overwhelmed with the loyal and kind acts of others, discover the facts and notice behaviors before attempting to offer a definite resolution. Perhaps at some point, using kind and gentle words could help ease the path to making friends and family aware that the bereaved needs some time alone. When done in an appropriate way by graciously thanking the well-wishers for their unselfish acts of kindness, it could offer grace and a needed break for the well-meaning family and friends.

Stages of Grieving

There are several stages in the grieving process that do not necessarily have to be in any particular order. From my experience, the following stages will be explored:

Anger

One denotation of anger is "a strong feeling or displeasure or hostility." Some people do not experience the anger aspect of grieving in a methodical or predetermined way. According to some clients, as one person expressed it, "I am truly hurt, and I know we all must die; therefore, I am not angry, but I am hurt because I miss him so much." Whether you are hurt or angry, they are both valid responses. In either case, it causes sadness and reduces the level of happiness. Anger should be watched and guarded closely because it could turn into bitterness, bitterness into hate, and hate into a possibly harmful situation. Hurt can be described as anger under control as described in the above quote. When facilitating a grieving session, try to discover the reason for the anger. What is the source of the anger? Some people experience anger when their breadwinner is lost and they feel inadequate to care for themselves. As one spouse declared, "Who will take care of me now?" Others might be angry because the joy of companionship is lost.

It is important to prepare for any conferencing session, especially when you know what type of session you will be facilitating. Be prepared to ask certain significant questions with appropriate sensitivity of the bereaved. It is important to recognize interests as well as issues when conferencing with the bereaved, whether it is a person or a family group. Recognize the various relationships within a group with the deceased. Treat everyone's emotions with respect and genuine sincerity. Be prepared to offer some assistance by providing sources of help to a person who has just lost a loved one. Whether a child loses a playmate or a teenager loses a friend, big sister or brother, be prepared to offer a suitable substitute, not as a replacement, but someone whom the bereaved can relate to and trust. After a death, there is a void and transition for you to make. Offering a substitute to ease the pain from the void of losing a loved one, could be well received by the bereaved if this is what is desired. Offering to provide a mentor through a mentoring program at church, school, or community services could prove helpful. If you do not have adequate or meaningful assistance at the time of the conference, take time and make notes of the needs of the bereaved and inform them you will be getting back at a later time with more information. This will help put the bereaved at ease and create an atmosphere of trust and genuine concern.

Often certain issues might be readily identifiable; however we have to look and listen for interests. A person's interest can be the reason for the issue. Interests are similar to values and should be treated with respect. An interest can be the driving force in a person's life so careful acknowledgement and recognition must be assured.

Denial

Explained by various definitions, denial is a refusal to comply. The most often used phrase I have heard as an immediate response is "I do not believe this has happened." Just this response alone is not an indication that someone is in denial; however when one continues to behave in a manner as if the deceased still exists, this would be cause to suspect denial. Clients have informed me that after the passing of their spouse, they, at times, placed two plates on the table at dinner time, but quickly removed one as their memory was jogged by recalling the death. To my understanding, this can happen quite often. I remember after the death of my sister, with whom I had a very close relationship, I even picked up the telephone to dial her number, then it dawned on me that she was no longer with me.

Based on my work experience and interacting with others, I am sharing these experiences to shed some insight into different and natural reactions to death. When someone continues to behave in a manner as if a deceased is still alive, for example, in the case of the wife placing two dinner plates on the table, but when a spouse, as I was told, actually expects to see her husband walk through the door, this is likely a form of denial.

Some spouses who have been left behind have their own way of coping with a spouse's death. One lady refused to sell her husband's car. Her response was, "I am just not ready. I like seeing his car in the garage." Another wife indicated that she could not take her husband's name off the checking account. Whatever the reason for people to behave as they do, the facilitator must be able to recognize that everybody does not function alike in the same time frame or in the same manner.

Depression

As defined by *Webster's New Universal Unabridged Dictionary,* depression is, "In psychology, an emotional condition either normal or pathological, characterized by discouragement, a feeling of inadequacy, low spirits, dejection, or sadness, etc." Based on this definition, initially after losing a loved one, it is a normal emotional condition that follows death. It is important to be aware of any behavioral changes while someone is experiencing depression. Studies show that suicidal tendencies can be traced to depression. It is recommended that you should call your doctor immediately when any unusual changes in behavior are noticed. Research further indicates by using antidepressants suicidal thoughts in children are increased. After conferencing with a client, I was informed by the client that before she had thoughts of suicide, she felt anger, depression, and rejection because her family had not supported her and acknowledged the work and service that she had given to the deceased. As a result, she went through periods of withdrawals, not wanting to talk or be around anyone. As a caretaker, friend or family member, if any unusual changes are noticed in the bereaved attitude or behavior, encourage medical or other necessary help. Early diagnosis and appropriate help can save lives.

Loneliness

Loneliness is a sense of being alone even when surrounded by others. According to one client, "It is an empty void that only one person could fill." Loneliness is a natural response after the death of a loved one. A person going through this phase of the grieving process should be encouraged to participate and interact with others. The facilitator should be not only sympathetic but empathetic as well when speaking and listening to the bereaved. Probing is a useful tool to help the bereaved to discover how the deceased life can be celebrated. Getting involved with a memorial or community service could serve to celebrate a life, and it brings the living back into circulation with other friends and the public.

Shock

A denotation of shock is the feeling of distress and disbelief that you have when something bad happens accidentally. An unexpected death, such as an accident or unusual illness, can leave beloved ones in a state of shock. Shock is sometimes short lived when one is able to accept the reality of a situation. When one dies suddenly with or without a known cause, loved ones are left with a sense of disbelief because he or she was here a few minutes ago and doing well and is now no more. Allowing loved ones to talk about how they feel about what happened by giving the time to wonder how this situation could have even happened, offers a time to exhale. A facilitator should schedule a time for allowing family members to just think aloud and express emotions in order to help them start the healing process. Usually, people do not always look for clad-in-iron answers when experiencing shock; rather they prefer someone to listen to them and just be there for moral and emotional support.

People desire time to ponder and express their thoughts of what if: "I wonder what might have happened. Could it have been prevented? Who could even do this to another person?" Just given the time to explore unanswered questions often soothes the emotions. When in shock, people desire details that are often not available. This stage offers the facilitator the opportunity to do some selective agreeing, a nodding of the head, and affirming certain statements made by a family member.

The facilitator should choose words wisely and meaningful to serve a purpose. Loose and untimely comments can often be counterproductive. The facilitator should always be alert to the physical as well as emotional condition of bereaved loved ones, and without hesitation inquire about professional or medical help with the family member if perceived help is necessary. You might ask if a particular family member is under medical or any professional guidance if there seems to be an indication this type of help is needed.

Adjustment and Healing

Adjustment can start immediately or within a short span of time with some people, and it might take a longer period of time to adjust to the death of a loved one with others. Depending on the emotions and needs of an individual, the period for adjustment is personal and should not be judged by the adjustment of others. Different people require different help or ways of coping. The healing stage usually starts when a person is able to start adjusting and accepting the death of a loved one. Being able to relate to people as they are, regardless of their religious orientation, denomination, pain, or circumstances can help ease their path to healing. Helping people where they are and accommodating their needs, spiritually physically and emotionally, will generally lead to a personal and healthful restoration.

Careful consideration should be given to young children and grandchildren when a parent or grandparent dies. Grandchildren hold a special and precious bond with grandparents and need the time and opportunity to express their emotions. Providing a special time for young children and grandchildren to express final thoughts of their beloved relationship promotes a loving and memorable closure. I have often heard the voice of grandchildren who desired to express and share their memories of love, gifts, and character of grandparents. Providing a special platform and time for children and grandchildren to openly grieve and memorialize a parent or grandparent can initiate the healing process. It is amazing to hear the thoughts and love expressed by teens and young children when given the opportunity to tell their own story about their own special relationship with the deceased. They talk about a very special time, event, or situation where their lives were significantly impacted. I have heard stories of how Grandma taught a young granddaughter how to make grandma's cookies. One young kid remembered the rides on Grandpa's back and how he and Grandpa played soft ball together, just the two of them. One child told of going to the ice cream store with Grandma and Grandpa. Pure and precious memories are often expressed through the mouths of babes.

Reflecting

Reflecting is often part of the healing process. One of my bereaved friends related that reflecting on the good times she and her husband once shared and thinking of the kind of person he was helped her to grow as a person. Edward, her deceased husband, once thought of as a miser by her and others, proved to be a very prudent man after death. My friend shared how she discovered a couple of insurance policies she knew nothing about; they named her as the beneficiary and were tucked away among some of his business papers. Another bereaved widow found pleasure in reflecting on the better qualities of the deceased rather than focusing of any shortcomings. After much consideration, many bereaved loved ones have continued the legacy of service following a loved one's death. As one source put it, "I still feel close to him when I am doing his work and using his imparted guidance and wisdom in order to help others."

Delayed Grieving

Death is generally looked upon as a finality or non-existent in respect to being part of our current world. When a person becomes missing in action or due to an unknown cause, whereabouts, or circumstances, these conditions can cause delayed grieving. Another situation that causes delayed grieving is a coexisting condition that requires immediate attention or focus. An example of a coexisting condition would be providing the duties of a caretaker or having sole responsibility for financial obligations without having the necessary means. A situation was shared with me by a bereaved spouse who had recently lost her father, a sister, and her husband. Immediately following the death of her husband, a daughter thought it would be helpful to bring her young child to comfort and live with her grandmother for an indefinite period of time. In the mind of the bereaved, being a *good* grandmother meant she should accept the child. After discussing the situation a while, the grandmother declared, "I feel as if I haven't had the time to grieve. I have been so busy taking care of my granddaughter until I do not have time to think much about my husband." The grandmother decided to give the child back to her mother in order that she could find peace and comfort with the loss of her husband.

When a loved one is missing in action, hope can often delay grieving. The hope of finding or locating the missing relative or friend is a present force that often redirects the focus of the emotions and attention. Not being prepared to readily accept death as a quick answer is a natural response for a missing loved one. Before accepting death, most loved ones prefer an identifiable body or forensic proof of death. Once death is evidenced by acceptable standards and legal proof, the grieving process can naturally begin.

Not having the necessary means to meet final arrangement financial obligations would be a reason to delay grieving because the mind is now occupied and focused on finding the necessary funds to satisfy certain expenses. When one dies unexpectedly and sometimes prematurely, it creates an untimely and unbudgeted expense if there has been no advanced planning to meet such needs. The facilitator should be sensitive with family members and to the pain that comes with the grieving process. Understanding the grieving process and it coexisting with external and unwanted forces, the facilitator should take measure to use the appropriate approach. Through careful probing, the client will usually reveal what issues are important to address at a particular time. The facilitator should stay mindful that grieving is not necessarily consistent with any given mold or blueprint used by others. Whatever a bereaved person or family wants in terms of being comforted or helped is what should be offered and addressed at the appropriate time. This does not prohibit the facilitator from exploring other support options if so deemed necessary.

Homework Assignment

Write a brief summary of this chapter, listing the principles and techniques taught in the text, being as specific as possible.

State how you plan to use some of the principles in your own life when facing similar situations or issues.

If you are involved in a group study, consider sharing your summary with other group members for discussion purposes.

Write a letter or prayer thanking God for what you have learned and how certain information has personally helped you.

"A man's wisdom gives him patience; it is to his glory to overlook an offense" (Proverbs 19:11, NIV).

CHAPTER SIXTEEN

Parental Conferencing

Parental conferencing is a dynamic process for engaging with parents or potential parents on the subject of parenting. The facilitator, as with other applications of the process, should remain neutral and without bias when conferencing parental issues. Each issue identified by the parents or potential parents should be given special attention and thorough review through probing and extensive dialogue. This chapter will explore and discuss common guidelines for positive and effective parenting. It is important that the facilitator (the parents at times) remains focused and mindful of the needs, issues, and interest of the parties involved in a conferencing opportunity.

Learning to parent starts very early in life. A child learns from his parents by both verbal and nonverbal communication whether it is positive or negative. A child sees before he speaks, and the brain is capable of recalling many things to our mind that we have stored in our memory, and it conveys to us how to act immediately especially when it is necessary to do so. I remember when I was a child walking along and alone on a narrow country lane, I walked upon a snake in a coiled position right at my feet, and without thinking, I jumped high and over the snake. I kept running until I was out of breath, and after taking a rest, I ran to my destination. My brain and action worked in concert without delay. Children often emulate attitudes, speech, and actions of their caretaker or whoever is the primary influence in their lives. Parents and caretakers are the most important influences in a child's life and have significant impact on molding their character and values through a controlled environment. Those who have had no formal training or acquired parenting skills tend to draw upon the skills demonstrated by their parents or caretakers. There is no definite blueprint for raising the perfect child; taking the necessary measure to learn what you do not know by seeking mature and trusting advice, and participating in a structured and reputable source of training, will ease the necessity of acquiring positive and effective parenting skills.

Pre-parenting Conferencing

Pre-parenting conferencing provides opportunities to explore important issues and interests and helps others to empower themselves through knowledge and understanding. Conferencing is open to helping a couple understand their desire to become parents, and it provides time to consider and recognize the obligations and privileges of parenthood.

Preparing for Parenthood

Preparing for parenthood is the first and most critical stage in parenting. Pre-parenting planning is just as important as acquiring parenting skills after becoming a parent. The first issue is *Am I ready to parent?* It takes more than a notion or a few thoughts on parenting in order to be an effective and nurturing parent. Certain requirements and considerations you should acknowledge and master before becoming a parent are:

1. Am I emotionally mature and stable enough to have children?

2. Do I have the necessary stability in my life at this time to have children?

3. Do I feel that my income is sufficient to sustain a viable, loving home environment?

4. Is my income sufficient to provide a home, clothing, shelter, food, and education for a child?

5. If I lose my job, are my skills sufficient to find another comparable or better job?

6. Do I have the time to devote to raising a child?

7. Am I physically ready to have a child?

8. Am I in good health?

9. Do I want to have a child before marriage or should I wait until after I am married?

10. Can I afford to provide for two families simultaneously, a home with my spouse and family and another home from a prior relationship?

11. What kind of spouse do I want to raise my children?

12. Have I determined expectations for my child, and am I ready to impart quality core values, emotional, spiritual, and moral support for a child?

13. What are my expectations for a spouse and parent for my child?

14. Am I capable of providing structure and discipline for a child?

15. Have I reached my personal goals sufficiently enough to advance to the stage of being an adequate, loving, and effective parent?

16. What are possible consequences of having a child before marriage?

17. What are my expectations of myself as a parent, and are my expectations for myself realistic and feasible enough to provide positive parenting?

18. Have I learned anything from others that I should guard myself against?

19. Do I want to have a child because this is something I want, or do I want a child in order to give my parents a grandchild?

20. Giving careful consideration and understanding the impact of each item listed, should give you significant insight into preparing for parenthood.

Parenting Children from a Previous Relationship

Both Pete and Gail brought a child from a previous relationship into their marriage. At the time of the conference, they had been married for fifteen years. From the outset of the conference, bitterness permeated their dialogue. A few times they were reminded of the conferencing guidelines that they agreed to accept. Pete told his story about how disrespectful Gail's daughter, Carrie, was to him, how she had taken over the whole house including entering his and Gail's private bathroom without prior notice or permission. Pete continued sharing what was happening in the home. As he prepared to dress for work, Carrie entered his and Gail's private bathroom to get dressed for school. When he approached Carrie and asked if she would kindly use the other bathroom, he described how she offered no verbal apology but just an unkind look, and with gyrations of the shoulders brushed him off. Pete continued to make Gail aware of the unacceptable practice of Carrie's attitude and behavior. Gail stated that she wanted Pete to correct Carrie's attitude without offering to help. Pete reminded Gail that he preferred her to instruct Carrie about her attitude and behavior because he was not comfortable doing so. Pete is known to be a big teddy bear type of guy. He disliked any type of confrontation especially with his daughter, and he was sure it would be a confrontation rather than a discussion with Carrie.

Gail took her turn in telling her own story. Gail was unhappy about the behavior of Tim, Pete's son from a previous relationship. She alleged that Tim did not give her proper respect and was a very untidy person. Gail told about Tim's refusal to do house chores and yard work. As a result of the bitterness, and lack of effective communication, the home was a wreck, both physically and emotionally. The home was in a state of total disorganization; no house rules, no particular job assignment to any particular person on any given day, no eating together, and everyone was going in his or her own direction.

After both Gail and Pete shared their stories, they were asked to share the type of relationship they had before marriage. Generally they had fun and enjoyed being together. Gail stated how she appreciated Pete's generosity with Carrie as well as with herself. Pete stated how loving and caring Gail was about doing certain things for him and his son. They both admitted that the failure to discuss or structure a plan for a happy family life resulted in a painful misunderstanding. Gail and Pete were tired of their present home life and the bitterness that kept them at odds with each other. They wanted a more peaceful life of harmony, love, and respect and were willing to work toward accomplishing this goal.

The following list gives a view of what Pete, Gail and the children were happy to implement in their home in order to establish a peaceful home environment.

Tips for a Structured Home Environment

1. A tidy and well-organized home is conducive to having a peaceful home life.

2. Identify and designate daily chores for family members.

3. Keep family dialogue in the home within the bounds of common courtesy.

4. Gail would instruct Carrie on improving her behavior and attitude toward Pete. This would include but not be limited to giving him proper respect and accommodating his instructions as long as they were honorable and helpful for the household.

5. Pete would instruct Tim on improving his attitude toward Gail and helping with daily chores.

6. The family members would exhibit kindness and gentleness toward each other.

7. Pete and Gail would establish what was allowed and disallowed in the home.

8. At a determined time, the parents would give to each child uninterrupted time for private discussions. For example, a trip to the child's favorite restaurant, a movie, a walk in the park—any acceptable time to allow the child to talk about his desires, goals, problems, or other personal issues.

9. From time to time review house guidelines and solicit ways to improve or modify them.

10. Create a family calendar applicable to all family members for structure, encouragement and acknowledgment of any good work.

11. Schedule a time for discussions to share expectations of each other with the understanding that goal setting starts at a very early age.

12. Discuss the importance of keeping an organized and tidy home.

13. Discuss the benefit of healthy eating habits.

14. Establish boundaries for the children.

15. Discuss acceptable manners and voice tones.

16. Explain the importance of using words to build up rather than to tear someone down.

17. Personal constructive criticism will be given in privacy.

18. Pete and Gail would plan a date with each other at least once a month.

Homework Assignment

Write a brief summary of this chapter, listing the principles and procedures taught in the text, being as specific as possible.

State how you plan to use some or all of the principles in your own life when facing similar situations or issues.

If you are involved in a group study, consider sharing your summary with other group members for discussion purposes.

What can you personally take from this chapter in order to help or share with others?

Write a letter or prayer thanking God for what you have learned and how certain information helped you.

"The tongue has the power of life and death, and those who love it will eat its fruit" (Proverbs 18:21 NIV).

CHAPTER SEVENTEEN

Bullying

"What causes fights and quarrels among you? Don't they come from your desires that battle within you?" (James 4:1, NIV)

Bullying is an inappropriate behavior that has been around for a long time. A bully is defined by *Webster's New Universal Unabridged Dictionary* as "A person who teases, hurts, or threatens smaller or weaker persons." Bullying, if not controlled or altered, can result in physical harm, emotional damage, or even death to another.

Let us review the story of Cain and Abel as told in the Bible. "Abel became a shepherd, while Cain was a farmer. At harvest time, Cain brought the Lord a gift of his farm produce, and Abel brought the fatty cuts of meat from his best lambs and presented them to the Lord. The Lord accepted Abel's offering but not Cain's. This made

Cain both dejected and very angry, and his face grew dark with fury. "Why are you angry?" the Lord asked him. "Why is your face so dark with rage? It can be bright with joy if you will do what you should! But if you refuse to obey, watch out. Sin is waiting to attack you, longing to destroy you, but you can conquer it!" One day Cain suggested to his brother, "Let's go out into the fields." And while they were together there, Cain attacked and killed his brother." But afterward the Lord asked Cain, "Where is your brother? Where is Abel?" "How should I know" Cain retorted. "Am I supposed to keep track of him wherever he goes?" (Genesis 4:2b– 4:9, The One Year Living Bible).

Abel was Cain's younger brother and perhaps weaker in strength due to their age difference. It is easy to assume that Abel could have been both physically and emotionally intimidated out of respect for an older sibling. Cain demonstrated poor judgment and a cowardly defense. When God asked him, "Where is your brother?" Cain did not give a straightforward answer; rather, he answered with another question: "Am I supposed to keep track of him where he goes?" A simple yes or no would have sufficed. Cain's response to God's question was a form of denial and a misrepresentation. Failure to acknowledge and accept responsibility and accountability for one's action are characteristics of a coward or bully.

Reclaiming your Power from the Bully

If you are hurting or still finding yourself being depressed due to you being bullied at some point in your life, you have the power to decide a decision; a decision that will be your personal commitment that will free you from the power of the person who bullied you. Realizing who a bully really is will help you understand that courage and self-discipline are not characteristics of a bully. Are you willing to allow a person with less courage than you consume your energy by giving him your power? You have the power to say, "No." The following information is useful when making a decision to rid you from the power of a bully:

1. Bullying is an unprovoked attack on an individual that is unwarranted and meant to cause harm.

2. A person who bullies demonstrates low self-esteem and a cowardly behavior.

3. Are you allowing yourself to be consumed by the acts of a bully?

4. What is it that you want stopped? Are you willing to decide that you are better than what you are allowing yourself to be? Are you ready to reclaim your power by changing your attitude about what happened in your life at a certain time?

5. Are you ready to say, "I will no longer surrender my mind and energy to a coward?"

6. Are you able to say, "I have decided that I am more than a pawn in the hand of a bully, and I am reclaiming my power through my faith and inner strength?"

Environments of Bullying

Bullying in the Schools

This story is the result of a one-on-one conversation I had with a parent, whom I will refer to as Jill, whose child was being bullied at school. I was attending a seminar on bullying at a local university, when I arrived early and was able to engage in small talk with other attendees. I was sitting near the front, left of the presenters' table when a young lady walked up to me. We chatted for a while, and after a brief and polite introduction, Jill began talking about the subject matter and asked, "What brings you to this seminar?" I gave her a brief scenario of my interest in the subject. Immediately Jill began to tell me her story as to why she was attending the seminar. Her son was being bullied on a daily basis at the school he attended. Tears welled up in her eyes as she talked about how he hated going to school each morning. Jill explained some mornings he complained of tummy aches—he could not finish his breakfast—and even cried at times.

Jill informed me that she had spoken with school officials several times but to no avail. After listening to Jill's scenario about how bullying was affecting her young son's life, I was able to empathize with her and was feeling her pain. I have a close relative who is a little younger than Jill's son, and I could only imagine if his life was being impacted by the behavior of a bully.

It was now time for class to start; however, I was not able to forget what Jill and I had talked about. During class time, my mind was bifurcated between what the speaker was saying and what Jill had told me. We talked about exchanging telephone numbers but were interrupted, as others were, by the speaker calling for attention.

Many personal stories, news articles and statistics document the harm of bullying. Parents have lost children who committed suicide because of being bullied. A local university experienced the *nightmare* of bullying when one of its students committed suicide after another student placed his personal affair on the Internet. Since suicide as a result of bullying is broadly documented, it is important that friends, family members, and associates be aware of its consequences. Give close attention to any unusual changes in behavior and attitude. If someone makes a change in attitude by withdrawing from social activities, friendly conversations, or not being available for any type of interaction with others, make your concern known to appropriate people whether it is a parent, teacher, a reliable friend, or professional. Getting help early could save a person's life. If you are being bullied, before taking your life, try talking to just one other trusted and reliable person. Giving your power to anyone who uses bullying to unjustly disturb your life is not a fair exchange by giving your own life. Do not enable bullies to continue bullying by succumbing to their cowardly, hurtful, and selfish acts. Schools are now more aware than ever of the devastation that bullying creates. Speaking with teachers and other school personnel, it was made clear that bullying is a major concern; programs have been implemented to minimize bullying. To help schools stop bullying, students are encouraged to report any bullying activities being carried out on school premises.

After class, I returned home and continued to ponder the look on Jill's face. Her voice tone and bewildered behavior etched an indelible spot on my heart. Jill's conversation inspired me to do whatever I could to ease the pain of bullying. I decided that since I was not able to significantly help Jill in such a short time, I concentrated of treating this one-on-one conference with the same respect and intensity that I would give to any conference that I would facilitate.

The following is a list of options that could be useful for evaluation and consideration when encountered by a case of bullying.

Things parents can do on behalf of a child

1. If you believe that your child is a bully, encourage him or her to stop.

2. Discuss the lawful consequences of harmful bullying.

3. Get help for your child if he or she cannot control bullying.

4. Have family discussion to talk about the impact of bullying on the person who bullies victim and respective family members.

5. Discuss the harm of bullying on both families when someone is hurt or harmed.

6. Before your child starts a new school, have a visit with school officials to determine if a "No bullying policy" is implemented.

7. Discuss if the school has a mentoring or buddy system in place for new students. If not, discuss the possibility of establishing a student mentoring policy in which a volunteer student will mentor a new student, and agree to participate in getting the policy implemented.

8. Join the PTA (Parent and Teacher Association) and work to get the subject of bullying on the school board's agenda.

9. Talk to your child and assist him or her with appropriate ways of dealing with a bully. Report any bullying or misbehaving to school officials.

10. Walk away from a bully, and do not be afraid to say, "Stop, I do not like what you are doing."

11. Once a child starts class, often the bully is easily recognized by his attitude. If possible, the child can minimize contact with the bully without having to give up any rights or privileges.

12. Instruct the child to report any bullying or personal harassing to school officials as soon as possible and to their parents.

13. Encourage your child to share with you any concerns he has that might be negatively impacting his life, or any uncomfortable demands made by another person.

14. Encourage the child not to be afraid to say "No" or "Stop" if asked to do something he is not comfortable doing.

15. If someone is doing something unkind to your child, encourage him to walk away and report it to a school official.

16. Encourage your child to walk away when there is opportunity to do so.

17. Comfort your child in knowing that he or she has the right to attend school free of intimidation and harassment.

18. Talk about the subject of suicide. Encourage your child to talk to you or some trusted person when he or she has thoughts of suicide.

19. Ask your child not to commit suicide, rather come to you and talk to you.

20. Encourage your child to be aware of his surroundings, especially people who initiate arguments or fights.

21. Encourage your child to be make new friends with whom he is comfortable.

22. Teach your children the importance of good character at an early age in order to enhance their awareness and discernment of inappropriate behavior.

23. Listen to your child's verbal and nonverbal communication.

24. If your child evades a question or is not straightforward with a desired answer, probing and open-ended questioning in a nonthreatening manner can uncover hidden feelings or fears of a threat.

25. Ask questions that require a narrative answer.

26. Seek to discover what the child is feeling and not just what is being said.

27. Know your child, check for bruises or bumps on his or her person.

28. Ensure your child that he is loved by his family.

29. Notice any change in attitude, behavior, or grades of your child.

30. Establish a chat time for just the two or three of you. (This is for both parents.)

Bullying with the aim to Intimidate

Bullying is a form of controlling that happens beyond the boundaries of schools. The act transcends any particular genre or category. It often impacts the home, church, workplace, community, and other groups and organizations. In homes where one family member intimidates other family members by keeping them fearful of the consequences of his or her displeasure, this is a form of bullying. One family's story was about how the family could find peace only when the father was away. The least little thing could set him off, such as a certain food prepared for dinner that he did not like; he would sometimes strike the wife or toss a plate across the kitchen. The wife was terrorized by his unpredictable anger. The husband's aggression would extend to taking away the car keys so the wife would not leave the house for any significant distance or he would limit her allowance to bare necessities to run the household by requiring receipts for any purchased item.

This type of bullying impacts the whole household. The young children, ages four and six, would cling to their mother's dress during the father's presence. When he was away, the kids found time to play. Due to fear of her husband's wrath, the wife was afraid to leave or seek the necessary help to abate the situation.

Bullying in the Church

You might wonder how someone in the church could be a bully or be bullied. Since bullying is a form of control, it can come in different and more subtle ways than being physical or confrontational. Cliques can lead to bullying. You have heard of cliques in junior high where several girls or boys come together to form a club or gang for the purpose of self-exaltation. Other goals of cliques with the intent to bully are: Excluding others, abiding by self-made rules and self-given entitlements. Since Scripture teaches to abstain even from the appearance of evil, church members should exercise careful planning when establishing certain boards, programs, and ministries. After conferencing with individuals who were disappointed with how their church structured its ministries and programs; it was clear that the church entrusted a lot of power to its directors of ministries without a check and balance to measure any effectiveness.

In the church, when cliques or the appearance of cliques are formed without malice or ill-intentions, conflict or discord can arise when friends are chosen to participate and others are omitted or overlooked. Controlling or unjustly eliminating the service of some members based on a personal dislike is a form of bullying. Disallowing a member to exercise a God-given talent is a form of controlling because it limits the member's ability to serve; moreover it denies others the value of benefiting from a particular talent or resource.

A church member explained that in order to minimize conflict and discord in the church that she attended, the leaders placed in use a process for keeping peace. The first initiative was, the pastor encouraged the congregation to love each other as God commanded us to do; secondly, a box was placed in a certain area where any member could place a comment or offer a service for the benefit of the congregation. If a member was hurt, ill or felt overlooked, he or she could place a note in the box requesting a conference with appropriate church officials to discuss this issue. A culture of peace in a church benefits all members. Many churches have peacemaking ministries that help the church body function in a culture of peace. The church is like a family, everybody wants to be loved, respected and included. This is helpful for having a happy family life and living in harmony.

Bullying in the Workplace

Bullying creates conflict thereby disharmony erupts into disputes. Many major companies now have in place a grievance procedure that allows disputes to be resolved through mediation or conciliation. Examples of bullying in the workplace could be disparity in job assignments or fear of subsequent retaliation from one who has been disciplined, whether it is an employee or manager. When a manager or someone in authority violates a company procedure by actions or words against an employee, or threatens the employee of unfavorable consequences if his actions are reported, is a form of bullying. An act that disallows an employee to work overtime due to a personal dislike is a form of bullying because another person's ability to earn something of value was taken.

A stronger person taking advantage of a weaker person by physical force or authoritative power is a form of bullying. The act of a supervisor taking credit for an employee's work as his own is bullying because the power vested in a supervisor comes with trust and integrity; this honor was violated, and the value of the work was unjustly taken from the employee.

Effects of Bullying

The effects of bullying can be long-lived with an indelible and painful memory etched in the hearts and minds of the bullied. Many adults have shared stories concerning how the abusive act of bullying invaded their lives. Some have told about how they have lived with low self-esteem because of being bullied as a child and as adult; some of these individuals still hold bitterness for the one who bullied them.

Bullying not only damages the one who is bullied, but also the one who is doing the bullying is impacted. Since becoming an adult, graduating from college, and getting married, one manager in the business world had regrets of bullying younger and weaker kids during his elementary and junior high years. His son was now being bullied in kindergarten and regretted going to school. After seeing the results of bullying his son was experiencing, he realized the pain he caused students at his school. The manager acknowledged that he wished he could apologize to the ones he bullied and let them know that he now sees them as being stronger than he was at that time. Some people bully others because of personal insecurities or feelings of inadequacy in their own lives. The business manager stated how he was unable to play basketball or football well enough to make the team. Even though his grades were average or better at times, he did not accomplish the one thing that he really wanted to do, which was playing sports—particularly football.

Six things to consider before bullying others

Consider how bullying would impact your life and how you would feel if someone in a higher authority or physically stronger would bully you.

Consider the impact, abuse and pain that bullying would cause someone and their family.

Consider who would benefit by being bullied or bullying others.

Consider how you would feel if your child, parent, or sibling was being bullied.

Consider alternative useful ways to vent your anger, bitterness, or insecurities.

Do not bully anyone.

Consider the immediate and future effects of bullying on the bullied and the bully.

Cyberbullying

At this juncture in our history, cyberbullying is the newest form of bullying because of its widespread use of technologies, particularly the Internet and cell phones. The "Cyberbullying Fact Sheet" authored by Sameer Hinduja, PhD, and Justin W. Patchin, PhD, defines cyberbullying as a "willful and repeated harm inflicted through the use of computers, cell phones, and other electronic devices."

Cyberbullying is painful, powerful, and it creates a permanent record through the use of cell phones, Internet, and various electronic devices. Its audience is much broader than the work place or any particular organization. At the click of the mouse or the proverbial *send* button, a cyber message can reach millions of people. The powerful act of cyberbullying often leaves permanent damage and even death upon its victims. It is fast traveling and difficult to control once it is on the Internet or sent by other uses of technology. Its victims are usually left feeling hurt, depressed, and helpless to abate the harm. Some victims have attempted or committed suicide in an effort to cope with the ugly act of bullying. Whereby gangs were generally considered the epitome of bullying, cyberbullying has taken the hurt and harm to a new level. Published news articles document the tattered effects of cyberbullying. A student studying at a university, body was recovered from the Hudson River after jumping off the George Washing Bridge. Allegedly, a private encounter was videotaped by another person and downloaded it on the Internet.

Grieving the death of a loved one is painful regardless if by violence or natural causes. However, through the comfort of family and loving friends, the grieving process is often given the dignity of privacy. Once the details that caused a death are exposed to public attention, the privacy element is taken away. The publicity can leave the pain of embarrassment for the family if death was due to an undesirable act of evil. Unlike when one dies from making a valiant or heroic effort to render a noble and useful service, the exposure to public attention is often acceptable and welcomed by the victim's family. Recognition of a good work is generally accepted and appreciated by the recipient and the family of the recipient as well.

Cyberbullying is a silent type of bullying that is often more powerful than physical bullying. The posting of private or personal information or even photographs taken in a compromising position on a public domain could cause emotional scars and personal embarrassment to the victim. The Bible teaches us to abstain even from the appearance of evil and to overcome evil with good (1 Thessalonians 5:22 and Romans 12:21). If people would just start thinking of not only their own interests but also the interests of others (Philippians 2:4), this would be a much kinder and gentler society.

Consequences of Bullying

The results of bullying can have a long and lasting effect. Both the bully and the bullied carry indelible scars internally and externally. The victims' emotions are damaged along with their, self-worth and confidence. Clients, whom I have worked with tirelessly, explain how their experience with being bullied still haunts them in their adult life. Having trouble trusting someone, easily intimidated, and the feeling of being not good enough are among the many side effects of being bullied. The bullies often look for ways to atone. One bully expressed that he wish he could find the person he bullied in grade school in order to offer an apology and ask for forgiveness. Some clients report that they have a feeling of bitterness attributed to being bullied. They feel angry and bitter for allowing themselves to be bullied even when the option to fight back was not an option. A child does not have the option to fight back or the resources. Laws of the land are made to protect the innocent.

One bully expressed that, as an adult, he still suffers from the hurt that he caused others by bullying them. He has regular medical care for depression. *As stated by one bully, "It is nothing like having to live with the guilt of having damaged someone by bullying them." Are you suffering from being bullied or having bullied someone, there is help available? Consider using the following tips given by offenders and victims of bullying to help you through your situation:*

1. Find some one you can trust, and talk about how you bullied others and what you were going through at the time.

2. Start trying to help others by teaching against bullying and sharing how bullying has affected your life.

3. Try to find the people you bullied in order to apologize and ask for forgiveness.

4. Acknowledge your participation in causing any harm.

5. Accept accountability for your actions.

6. Encourage others not to entertain thoughts of bullying.

7. Confess your sin before God.

8. Forgive yourself.

9. Share your experience of bullying with others.

10. If you are bullying others, *just stop.*

11. Remember the Law of Harvest: *"Be not deceived; God is not mocked: for whatsoever a man soweth, that shall he also reap," Galatians, 6:7 the JKV.*

Scripture teaches that, *"If we confess our sins, he is faithful and just to forgive us our sins, and to cleanse us from all unrighteousness," 1John, 1:9, the KJV.*

How Teens can deal with Cyberbullying

Sameer Hinduja and Justin W. Pachin (2010). Activities for Teens: Ten Ideas for Youth to Educate their Community about Cyberbullying.
Cyberbullying Research Center (www.cyberbullying.us). Several of these ideas are presented in this text.

"Research the problem. Spend time online to obtain a solid understanding of cyberbullying. Make notes on what you learn, and think about other related aspects, such as its causes and consequences.

Arrange Interviews with experts. Develop questions to ask cyberbullying experts. Find them online, in libraries, and then send them an email or give them a call to learn more about this problem.

Create information posters which can be prominently displayed throughout the school. Use vivid colors and imaginative slogans to bring attention to cyberbullying and how to deal with it.

Develop a website, blog, or Face book group. Create an online resource for your friends and community by summarizing cyberbullying and linking to valuable information elsewhere on the Internet. Remember to give credit for information you obtained from other sources and ask for use permission if necessary.

Establish a student mentoring program. Ask your former teachers or principals from middle and elementary schools if you could talk to their students about cyberbullying. Share with them your experiences and ideas on how to keep safe online, and tell them what to do if they run into trouble. They value your opinion more than you might think."

Using Circular Conferencing to Deal with Cyberbullying

Circular conferencing is an effective physical seating formation to use when discussing or facilitating issues of disputes or general issues of concern. It provides ease of eye contact with other participants, and it provides an atmosphere of equal value. It eliminates the perception of an authoritative position and is conducive for adding consideration and value to all who wish to be heard. Using the same format recommended for conferencing as described previously in this text, it provides a nonthreatening but welcoming environment to discuss issues of concern where opinions might differ significantly among the participants. This process provides benefits for both parties. It offers an opportunity for the victim to come face to face with the offender. The victim has the privilege of asking the offender relevant questions pertaining to the offense. It often gives the victim a better insight into understanding how the offender got to the point of becoming a bully.

The conferencing process provides the offender the opportunity to talk directly to the victim. If the offender so wishes, he can ask the victim for forgiveness and express any remorse for committing the offense. Once the offender and the victim have revealed an inner view of themselves, as to who they are by expressing their personally held perceptions and core values, the healing process for both parties is sometimes started during the conferencing. In some cases, the healing process for the victim is delayed until the victim is emotionally ready or able to cope with the offense. Some victims want to see a change in the offender. They want to see whether the offender will comply with the terms of the agreement to heal the harm. The victim wants to see the offender do something that is constructive and positive, such as going back to school, enrolling in an anger-management course, or some other activity or study that would help the offender become a better person.

When discussing the issues of bullying, particular cyberbullying, it is necessary to discuss the following concerns:

1. Discuss the impact of cyberbullying on both the bully and the victim.

2. Talk about how cyberbullying impacts the family and community.

3. Discuss why people would want to bully someone else.

4. If you have been the victim of cyberbullying, share with the group how it made you feel.

5. Be proactive about dealing with cyberbullying.

6. Talk to faculty members about inviting a trained facilitator on the subject of bullying to come and talk to the students about cyberbullying.

7. Discuss cyberbullying and its impact at home with family members.

8. Talk to church administrators to gain their insight or willingness to participate in group conferences with the youth department.

9. Discuss the harm that bullying causes.

10. Discuss ways to stop all bullying by making a personal commitment not to bully anyone and encourage others not to bully anyone.

Other Forms of Bullying

Since bully is defined as "a person who teases, hurts, or threatens smaller or weaker persons," other forms of bullying might be found in the use of *authority by virtue of position, racism, and discrimination.* When one uses an authority that is superior in rank than a subordinate position with the intent to disfavor or harm a particular individual, this is a form of bullying because it is taking advantage of a weaker or smaller person who has less power or authority. This can be done by disallowing or not giving rightful credit of a good work to a person performing at a lower position. Disparity in payment for the same job is a form of bullying, by paying a different compensation to different people, unless there is a clear understanding as to why the disparity is allowed.

When a hate crime is committed due to racism, this is a form of intentional harm and can be classified as bullying because the intent to harm is considered. One definition of discrimination, as offered by *Merriam-Webster's Intermediate Dictionary*, is "to treat some people better than others without any fair or proper reason (*discriminated against because of their race*). To discriminate with the intent to deny, disallow, or discredit are forms of bullying when it is against an innocent person or group with a disparity in power or position. Using blackmail as a force of power to control or expose an individual by publicly revealing personal or private information that might impose an adverse side effect upon the victim is a form of bullying when used to accomplish a personal gain by the blackmailer.

Homework Assignment

Write a brief summary of this chapter, listing the principles taught, being as specific as possible.

State how you plan to use some of the principles in your personal life when facing similar situations or issues as a victim or facilitator.

If you are involved in a group study, consider sharing your summary with other group members for discussion purposes.

Write a letter or prayer thanking God for what you have learned and how certain information has helped you.

List other forms of bullying that are familiar to you.

"Do not be overcome by evil, but overcome evil with good" (Matthew 18:16, NIV).

CHAPTER EIGHTEEN

Foundations of Conflict

Conflict with Your Spirituality

Conflict with your spirituality exists when God's law is violated. When man rejects the redemptive work of God through Christ by not accepting His plan of salvation, conflict is created between him and God. In a perfect place, the Garden of Eden, conflict existed. After His creation of male and female, God placed them in the garden of Eden with specific instructions, and God commanded the man by saying, "From any tree of the garden you may eat freely; but from the tree of the knowledge of good and evil you shall not eat, for in the day that you eat from it you shall surely die" (Genesis 2:16–17, NAST).

"Now the serpent was craftier than any beast of the field which the Lord God had made. And he said to the woman, 'Indeed, has God said, 'you shall not eat from any tree of the garden'?

And the woman said to the serpent, 'From the fruit of the trees of the garden we may eat; but from the fruit of the tree which is in the middle of the garden, God has said, 'You shall not eat from it or touch it, lest you die.' And the serpent said to the woman, 'You surely shall not die! For God knows that in the day you eat from it your eyes will be opened and you will be like God, knowing good and evil.'"

When the woman saw that the tree was good for food, and that it was a delight to the eyes, and that the tree was desirable to make one wise, she took from its fruit and ate; and she gave also to her husband with her, and he ate." (Genesis 3:1–6, NAST).

According to Scripture, there was conflict between God and Satan, who was the "anointed cherub." But Satan, according to Isaiah, 14:13–17 NAST, created conflict because he planned in his heart to revile against God. "But you said in your heart, 'I will raise my throne above the stars of God, and I will sit on the mount of assembly in the recesses of the north. I will make myself like the Most High,' nevertheless, you will be thrust down to Sheol, to the recesses of the pit. Those who see you will gaze at you, they will ponder over, saying, 'Is this the man who made the earth tremble, who shook kingdoms, who made the world like a wilderness, and overthrew its cities?'"

Satan departed from the way of the Lord because he wanted to be like God; therefore he was defeated by God and thrown out of heaven.

"You were the anointed cherub, who covers, and I placed you there, you were on the holy mountain of God" (Ezekiel 28:14, NAST).

Consequences

There are consequences when God's law is violated. As a result of Adam and Eve's disobedience and the cunning efforts of the serpent, all three were cursed. "And the Lord God said to the serpent, "Because you have done this, cursed are you more than all cattle, and more than every beast of the field; on your belly shall you go, and dust shall you eat all the days of your life; and I will put enmity between you and the woman." To the woman, He said, "I will greatly multiply your pain in childbirth, in pain you shall bring forth children; yet your desire shall be for your husband, and he shall rule over you." To Adam, He said, "Because you have listened to the voice of your wife, and have eaten from the tree

about which I commanded you saying,' you shall not eat from it,' cursed is the ground because of you; in toil you shall eat of it all the days of your life"
(Genesis 3:14–17).

"Do not be deceived, God is not mocked; for whatever a man sows, this he will also reap" (Galatians 6:7, NAST).

Conflict with Relationships

Conflict with relationships stems from a sea of reasons. It starts when two or more people are at odds or disagreement with each other. Conflict with others can arise from a myriad of sources. The root of disputes can originate with a general dislike or disrespect for another person. Envy or jealousy can be the root cause of conflict with others. A general and more common cause of conflict with others is by a misunderstanding or miscommunication with someone about something that was said or done.

Perception is a more subtle, but often a primary cause of conflict. When perceptions are used to determine a view of a situation without all the facts, it creates a breakdown in communication. Perceptions are real and sometimes painful to the person holding them; however perceptions are not necessarily factual. It is best to ascertain as much factual information as possible before making a decision based on innuendos and beliefs. Being open to hearing all sides of a dispute and evaluating the issues concerned, offer a path for mutual agreement. Many disputes can hinge on a misguided belief unless a clear understanding is reached.

Insufficient information as well as miscommunication is another crucial element for conflict. When insufficient information or incorrect instructions are acted upon as a guide for duty, the results are negative because the basis for the duty was not clear. Faulty directions or instructions will lead to a dissatisfactory outcome.

The restorative, circular conferencing process is ideal for resolving conflict with others because it allows the participants to work and sort through issues that have been clouded by misrepresentations while good intentions might be evidenced. The restorative conferencing process seeks to encourage and empower the participants to reach their own resolution through probing, getting a better understanding of the other person, and evaluating options to reach a mutual resolution without any undue duress from a third party.

Conflict with Circumstances

Conflict with circumstances can easily go unnoticed unless one is sensitive to the issues surrounding the conflict. Generally if a relationship has endured healthy attitudes during difficult situations, it is easy to assume that the participants are willing to discuss issues in a reasonable manner rather than placing blame from the outset. During hard economic times when loss of jobs are at an all-time high, financial circumstances seem to be a primary cause for many relationships, including but not limited to marriages. Business partners, friendships, and other relationships all suffer the financial pinch from an unstable economy.

Other circumstances can evolve from not knowing when to make a certain decision. A client wanted to purchase a home in a better neighborhood so her young child could go to a certain school. A delayed purchase would have been better for the client because this would give more time to save a more substantial down payment. The client's child had not reached regular school age. Purchasing in a depressed market generally comes with a better interest rate. In this case, the circumstance was to get a better interest rate or to wait and have a substantial down payment. This was a personal decision that was made when faced with this circumstance. Deciding the best solution to this scenario would be weighed on different factors for different individuals.

When making a decision as to what is best, evaluating the pros and cons for each issue and then considering the consequences for each action can lead to a resolution that is more comfortable and safer.

Conflict with Emotions

Whether it is anger, hurt, or disappointment, bruised emotions disturb your peace. Being in conflict with your emotions is a consideration that at times is too often overlooked as being a cause for conflict. From the start, it is easy for you not to see how your emotions can be the basis for certain conflicts due to your personal involvement. Over a span of fourteen years or more, after facilitating hundreds of cases, I find that people want their positions to prevail over others because they perceive their assumptions are just and correct. Since emotions are numerous, this text will discuss a few of the ones that are perceived to be more visible and identifiable.

Anger

Uncontrolled anger can lead to adverse and harmful consequences when acted out. The *Oxford English Dictionary* defines emotions as "Any agitation or disturbance of mind, feeling, passion; any vehement or excited mental state."

Anger is an emotion that is sometimes readily identifiable. It can occur quickly but at times can be delayed. An example that might cause immediate anger is using a perceived "hush, hush" word at the wrong time and in the wrong place, such as describing one's physicality or culture in a negative way. Having facilitated many conferences where someone rushes to a conclusion without having all the facts, mistakes and misjudgments are made. Making premature or irrational decision based on insufficient information can cause anger from an opponent, and it delays a peaceful resolution. Some people possess the propensity to control their anger better than others. These are the ones who will listen to the views and opinions of others, evaluate the issues and interests, and seek more information by using probing questions before deciding a conclusion. Daniel Goleman, as discussed in *"Managing Emotions", contends that knowing who you are and how to handle your emotions appropriately is built on how well you know yourself. Self-awareness allows you to overcome emotional setbacks quicker than people without* this ability.

Being able to handle emotions, especially explosive emotions, is helpful in gaining and maintaining peace. A peaceful relationship or environment is generally based upon the participants' ability to control sensitive emotions while seeking truth and facts to understand the position and interest of others.

Forgiveness

The act of forgiving is more beneficial to the person giving the forgiveness than the one who is receiving forgiveness. A few benefits of forgiving are the following:

Strength, which gives the forgiver the strength to go forward without being weighted down with the burdens of anger, bitterness, and hurt.

*Freedom, f*orgiveness frees the forgiver. It releases you from the control of the forgiven. Holding grudges, anger, or bitterness against another, because of not being able to forgive, keeps you in bondage and under the influence of the offender.

*Power, n*ot being able to forgive another is giving your power to others by allowing them to assume your thoughts, time, and energy. Being unable to forgive is like locking yourself up in jail and giving the key to an enemy.

Forgiving ourselves is just as important as forgiving others. Forgiving yourself helps you to go forward and releases you from your own bondage of breathing and thinking of your sins hourly and daily. Scripture teaches us to confess your sins, according to 1John, 1:9: "If we confess our sins, he is faithful and just and will forgive us our sins, and purify us from all unrighteousness" (The Student Bible, New International Version).

Forgiving others is so important that it impacts your own sins being forgiven by God. "Therefore, I tell you, whatever you ask for in prayer, believe that you have received it, and it will be yours. And when you stand praying, if you hold anything against anyone, forgive him, so that your Father in heaven may forgive you your sins," Mark, 11:24-25. "If I had cherished sin in my heart, the Lord would not have listened; but God has surely listened and heard my voice in prayer" (Psalm 66:18).

Bitterness

According to *Webster's New Universal Unabridged Dictionary*, bitterness is defined as a noun: "The state or quality of being bitter; figuratively, extreme enmity; sharpness; severity of temper; painful affliction, harshness, spite, grief, and distress."

Bitterness is not of benefit to anyone. It can cloud judgment and put enmity between involved parties. The Bible instructs to "Love your neighbor as yourself" (Leviticus 19:18). Scripture further encourages you to offer grace to others. "See to it that no one misses the grace of God and that no bitter root grows up to cause trouble and defile many" (Hebrews 12:15). Based on this scripture, you might say that bitterness can be a root cause for other emotional pain, trouble, and conflict steeped in the effects of bitterness. Bitterness can originate from a feeling of being hurt emotionally by someone. Some clients have shared that they build up an emotional or invisible wall that only the ones who are allowed by the alleged victim can penetrate this wall. Bitterness can lead to indifference if not dealt with in an appropriate manner through prayer, therapy, or the will to make a decision to release the hurt or harm perceived.

Hate

Hate is defined as "A strong feeling of dislike; to have a strong feeling of disgust, to find distasteful." Through conferencing, many people have proclaimed, "I do not love him. I do not want him or her, and even I hate her or him". These types of attitudes must be carefully facilitated. The facilitator might seek to find common ground that appeals to both parties. This could be the welfare of children or some other issue that may have been mentioned during a discussion. Remain careful not to take sides or place blame on either party. Help them to recognize the inner power of themselves, and encourage them to consider what would be best for each and all concerned. Reminding participants of biblical principles while seeking accountability from each party usually leads to profitable discussions.

Hate is a very strong word and must be regarded and respected when engaged in any dialogue. The use of the word *hate* can be explosive and counterproductive in trying to reach a degree of harmony and mutual respect. The participants in a conference should be encouraged to refrain from using any inflammatory words or phrases due to the possibility of harming and possibly causing damaged emotions unnecessarily.

Peace with God

Just as there are consequences when there is conflict with your spirituality, conversely there are benefits in having peace with God. A benefit of having peace with God is having the peace *of* God that follows. Having the peace of God is gained after having peace with God. Accepting the redemptive work of Christ, the shedding of His blood for all, and His resurrection give you peace with God. Having peace with God does not mean that he will grant everything that is on your prayer  list—your prayer must be in accordance with His will. However we can have peace in knowing that the Holy Spirit intercedes for us and takes our prayers to God according to His will. Romans, 8:26 and 27 state, "In the same way, the Spirit helps us in our weakness. We do not know what we ought to pray for, but the Spirit himself intercedes for us with groans that words cannot express. And he who searches our hearts knows the mind of the Spirit, because the Spirit intercedes for the saints in accordance with God's will" (NIV).

Having peace with God gives us eternal life. "God so loved the world that he gave his one and only Son, that whoever believes in him shall not perish but have eternal life" (Romans, 8:23, NIV). Peace with God gives us the assurance of many divine promises. "If we confess our sins, He is faithful and just to forgive us our sins and to cleanse us from all unrighteousness" (1 John, 1:9).

"The fruit of righteousness will be peace; the effect of righteousness will be quietness and confidence forever." Isaiah, 32:17 "Though the mountains be shaken and the hills be removed, yet my unfailing love for you will not be shaken nor my covenant of peace be removed." Isaiah, 54:10. There are many other precious promises that are spiritually beneficial and helpful. Taking the time to learn these Scriptures through Bible study, personal meditation, and study time will be a rich source of comfort, confidence, and encouragement.

The following testimonies have been shared by several people revealing their experiences and beliefs based on their personal peace with God:

California Minister and Naval Officer

"There will come a time in our lives where we will be faced with an experience or situation in which we have absolutely no control or influence over the outcome. It is at this point that we come face to face with the fact that we need God, and only He can do what is needed. This will require great trust and faith to sustain us through whatever the situation is. God uses these situations to check and see where we really stand with Him. Do we really trust him the way we profess to trust him to our friends and family, or is our faith based on talk?"

Senior Financial Officer

"I was driving home alone from my husband's high school reunion. I was planning to pick him up from a friend's house the next morning so that no one would drive under the influence of any substance. I was driving the speed limit on a dark suburban road, just north of the entrance to a very exclusive country club. While driving more than fifty miles an hour, the driver of a black SUV sped out of the country club driveway and exited without stopping to look either way. Had I been passing in front of that driveway entrance just a few seconds earlier, I would have been hit on the driver's side by this speeding SUV.

"I was very stunned to say the least. The SUV crossed my path like a flash of light. Even now, I still believe God's intervention saved my life; I know it. If I had been hit, and even if I lived, I would have been severely injured, and the SUV driver, perhaps, may not have even been injured or known the damage he had caused."

Educator

"During my time of illness, even before my doctor knew what was wrong with my head, I would lie awake at night wondering what was wrong with me and pray that God would reveal to me why my head was hurting so badly. One night I got out of bed and went into my living room, got behind a large chair, and began to cry and pray. My crying and praying left me weak. I got up from the floor, I do not remember when it happened, but I began to read my Bible looking for an answer. My search landed on Psalms, 56:8: 'You have seen me tossing and turning through the night. You have collected all my tears and preserved them in your bottle. You have recorded every one in your book.' My heart seemed to stop. I gasped and said, 'He knows.'

In my worst pain, joy flooded my soul. I know that God knows all things and that nothing is hidden from Him, but we have a tendency to think that God has something more important to do, more important than we are. What is more important to Him, than his own children? God knows and God cares for me. Remember you are never alone when you are in God's hands."

History Teacher

"When I am at my lowest, the doctors have grim hope for my recovery, and I have no compass to find a remedy, I know I can call on the Master and there I will have peace. I was at such a point in my life, and, having peace with God through His grace, he sustained me. I am happy to share this with others."

Administrative Educator

"I know that God hears and answers His children when they cry out to him. One day, I received a telephone call that my son, who lives hours away, was very ill and depressed. Not knowing what to expect on my arrival, I began to pray to God. He gave me a calming peace that enabled me to drive for at least four hours at night in the rain without losing control. I knew that He was with me and He was with my son. Only God can give unexplainable peace that passes our understanding."

Legal Counsel

"A memorable experience of having the peace of God is related to a difficult boss and having confidence that God is in control of things even while I am going through difficult times. A job experience with a certain employer was very difficult, one that I prayed about sometimes hourly. I was looking for an exit strategy which involved having another job before I left my position.

When our relationship became irreparable, I thought, and I was given the opportunity to stay or leave with acceptable compensation; I jumped at this option. I had faith that God's plan was something better for me. Since the timing was right, just the beginning of summer, I used this time to spend quality time with my family. Before the summer was over, I was offered another job that was a better fit for me and my family. This experience helped me to remain confident and know that when things get tough and are not going to plan, "We know that in all things God works for the good of those who love him, who have been called according to His purpose" (Romans 8,:28 NIV).

Restorative Facilitator

"My peace with God is confirmed by the Word of God, but an experience I encountered affirmed my peace. About 15 years ago, I was doing volunteer mediation work for a county mediation service. I was informed by another mediator that I needed to know some judges in order to get work from the Civil Courts. As I was leaving the building where I had helped resolve a case, the executive director invited me to a dinner on behalf of its volunteer mediators. I thanked him and asked where the dinner would be held. The director being aware that I did not care for driving at night, said, "Bring your husband with you."

My husband and I arrived at the site, the place was dimly lit and we did not see anyone immediately. A few minutes later, we noticed a dignified, mature-looking gentleman walking near the building where we were, wearing a black suit. My husband pulled our car close enough to speak with him. He inquired about the mediators' dinner, and the gentleman responded, "I am looking for the same dinner." Without being familiar with this person, my husband invited him to ride with us around to the other side of the building. While in the car, the gentleman introduced himself to us, and we told him who we were. The gentleman asked, "Who is the mediator", my husband told him about me. I informed him that I was told I could meet some judges at this dinner, and I had mailed some letters introducing my service to a few judges. He further inquired what judges I sent my letters. I began to give him some names, and when I got to his name, I will always remember what he said, "I'm he." At that moment, he invited me to send him my resume. Within two weeks, I received my first three cases for pay. I knew this was providentially arranged. Having not met any judges since receiving my certifications to mediate, and now having a judge in the back seat of our car, this was not only an affirmation of my peace with God, but also my calling."

Homework Assignment

Write a brief summary of this chapter, listing the principles and procedures taught in this text, being as specific as possible.

State how you would apply some of the principles in your own life when facing a similar situation or challenge.

If you are involved in a group study, consider sharing your summary with other group members for discussion purposes.

Write a letter or prayer thanking God for what you have learned and how certain information helped you personally.

Based on information in the text, write a personal opening statement for facilitating a restorative conference.

INSPIRATIONAL POETRY

"Pleasant words are a honeycomb, sweet to the soul and healing to the bones," (Proverbs, 16:24 NAST).

The author was inspired to write these poems
after hearing stories told by clients.
Inspirational Poetry

When

When you purpose in your heart
To do what's right no matter how hard,
That's honesty.
When you help some weary soul, whether a friend or a foe,
That's a neighbor.
When you ache for another's pain
And you lend a helping hand,
That's compassion.
When you judge another by truth and facts,
And you wish to be judged the same,
That's justice.
When you accept another's difference,
And you share their joy and pain,
And your love has no end,
That's a friend.
When you want to do what's best
To move ahead with your life,
And you forgive without forgetting,
That's righteous.
When you give your life to save another,
You suffer shame and pain,
With me and others on Your mind,
That's grace divine.

Beauty Is Not Hard to Find

When looking for beauty,
Keep an opened mind.
Outer beauty is fine,
Inner beauty is of a special kind.
Beauty is not hard to find,
And it is not confined to a period of time.
Strength and stature adorn the oak tree.
Power and calmness mystify the great seas.
Sobriety dignifies the soul,
Variety beautifies the seasons,
And the eye beholds beauty
For various reasons.
Beauty is not hard to find;
It is very precious in the eye of the blind.
It is more than just an outward shine.
True beauty is gloriously divine.

Living in Harmony

Face each day with a smile,
And before criticizing others
Walk in their shoes just one mile.
Accept that people are not all the same,
But know our differences are for our gain.
Before disliking others who might be slightly different,
Try to accept the challenge,
And make it a personal enrichment.
Understand they are no better or worse—
That might make us better persons.
Those who are different,
You should want to know,
Together you can stand a mighty blow,
Love others as yourself,
Do not stop if others rest.
If we all were equal and free,
What a wonderful world this would be.
If we want to live in harmony,
I must let it begin with me.

A Kitchen Prayer

Lord bless my kitchen to be a place to eat,
For friends, family, and strangers too.
Help me to welcome some weary soul
Who might be passing through.
Thank you Lord, for this lovely place,
Bless it abundantly with your grace,
Before we eat this food of the land,
Thank your Lord for your providing hand.

"Do not forget to entertain strangers, for by so doing some have unwittingly entertained angels" (Hebrews 13:2).

A Stranger at My Door

Hardship and pain without regard,
Establish kinship in every man's heart.
A common bond for mankind true,
One never knows when his is due.
A stranger or friend, we all are akin,
Not just by blood, gender, or skin,
It all has to do with making amends.
A stranger at my door
I know now she was a friend,
My sweetest gift another bore,
Was offered as a gift at my door.
A child was born without a home,
The mother pondered what went wrong,
To escape the pain, she made some gain,
She loved this child just the same.
A stranger at my door,
I did not even know,
She gave me a precious child and left with a smile.
She promised to return after a while.
I took this child not knowing any more,
From a stranger at my door.

A Wedding Poem

Today, I fulfill my betrothal and my love surrendered, too.
Before God and man, I commit my vows to you.
Full clouds in due season, I cannot promise,
My silver lining of love is yours eternally.
With this ring, I pledge thee my love.
O ring where does your circle end?
So far yet, no one has found,
This ring is like my love for you,
Neither one has placed any bounds,
Tomorrow might bring sunshine or rain,
Through storms and trials, we must remain.
On God's Word our foundation is laid,
In His care we know we are saved.
My heart and life I commit to thee,
With God as our witness,
May our true love ever be.

O Wretched Man I Am

O wretched man I am.
Darkness and emptiness embrace me,
My complaint is ever before Thee,
My days are consumed by memories and
Dreams of the night.
Deception creeps in on kitten feet, but,
With hands of talons, clutches its prey
Without warning.
O wretched man I am
So unworthy, so self-consumed,
Allow this wickedness not to be.
I am not in bondage; I've been made free,
I will now awake and honor Thee.
There is hope for me, I know.
I will remember His precepts and His promises.
His love shall sweeten the bitter pain of my stomach,
And my anxieties will cease in His care.
I ask for forgiveness for my doubting heart.
My soul is secure, and my eternity is sealed,
And, by faith, I will be like Him
When I see Him as He is.

Thoughts of a Christian Servant
A Poem for Retirement

A worthy servant can hardly retire,
The harvest is plentiful and the workers are few,
I still have gifts that must produce.
Serving is my calling, obedience is my charge,
My joy is in submission, because
His grace is so sufficient.
Sometimes a servant needs to rest,
In order to do his calling just,
The sun rises in the east and sets in the west;
I just want to give my best.
A worthy servant can hardly retire,
Someone needs to be reconciled,
For those He calls, He justifies,
Then I can retire when together in Christ,
We are both glorified.

Tell my Mamma that I love her

After serving as a surrogate parent, I was
inspired to write this poem:

When we awoke this morning, she had already left,
Little Johnny's eyes told how he felt.
No good buy kiss not even a hug,
Off to school to learn today,
O what's the use, I can't concentrate.
Tell my mamma that I love her.
Home again with my next of kin,
I miss my mamma, she's my friend.
Tell my mamma that I love her.
One week now, no word not even a call,
I dodged the gangs and got home safe,
I just know it was by His grace.
Tell my mamma that I love her.
Two weeks now, mamma's still gone,
O why was I ever born?
I believe some how some day
Momma will be straight, if by grace
It's not too late.
Tell my mamma that I love her.

Say Something

I am young and impatient,
I know who I am and what I want to do.
I did not choose to be born,
And the world owes me what is due.
Mistakes, I don't comprehend,
Wisdom is for those who pretend.
This was my former state of mind,
Before my life was on the line.
Now, I listen to wisdom,
If you see me traveling the wrong way,
Say something.
It is too costly to live and hate.
If I am about to make a mistake,
Say something before it's too late.
Life is more than just my way,
Don't take my life for me to repay.

Life Application Scriptures

Scriptures for Guidance and Encouragement
(The New International Version Bible)

1Corinthians, 10:31 – "So whether you eat or drink or whatever you do, do it all for the glory of God."

Romans, 12:18 – "If it is possible, as far as it depends on you, live at peace with everyone."

Psalms, 32:10b – "Many are the woes of the wicked, but the Lord's unfailing love surrounds the man who trusts in him."

Colossians, 3:13 – "Bear with each other and forgive whatever grievances you may have against one another. Forgive as the Lord forgave you."

Philippians, 4:4–7 – "Rejoice in the Lord always. I will say it again, rejoice. Let your gentleness be evident to all. The Lord is near. Do not be anxious about anything, but in everything, by prayer and petition, with thanksgiving, present your requests to God, and the peace of God, which transcends all understanding, will guard your hearts and your minds in Christ Jesus."

Matthew, 7:5 – "You hypocrite, first take the plank out of your own eye, and you will see clearly to remove the speck from your brother's eye."

Philippians, 2:4 – "Each of you should look not only to your own interests, but also to the interest of others."

Proverbs, 19:11 – "A man's wisdom gives him patience; it is to his glory to overlook an offense."

Proverbs, 3:5–6 – "Trust in the Lord with all your heart and lean not on your own understanding; in all your ways acknowledge him, and he will make your paths straight."

James, 4:1 – "What causes fights and quarrels among you? Don't they come from your desires that battle within you?"

Proverbs, 28:13 – "He who conceals his sins does not prosper, but whoever confesses and renounces them finds mercy."

Ephesians, 4:15 – "Instead, speaking the truth in love, we will in all things grow up into him who is the Head, that is, Christ."

Proverbs, 19:17 – teaches, "He who is kind to the poor, lends to the Lord and He will reward him for what he has done."

Matthew, 18:15 – "If your brother sins against you, go and show him his fault, just between the two of you. If he listens to you, you have won your brother over."

Matthew, 18:16 – "But if he will not listen, take one or two others along, so that every matter may be established by the testimony of two or three witnesses."

Romans, 12:21 – "Do not be overcome by evil, but overcome evil with good."

Matthew, 5:23–24 – "Therefore, if you are offering your gift at the altar and there remember that your brother has something against you, leave your gift there in front of the altar. First go and be reconciled to your brother; then come and offer your gift."

2nd Peter, 3:18 – "But grow in the grace and knowledge of our Lord and Savior Jesus. To him is the glory both now and forever."

James, 3:18 – "Peacemakers who sow in peace raise a harvest of righteousness."

Matthew, 19:26 – "James looked at them and said, 'With man this impossible, but with God all things are possible.'"

Romans, 5:1–2 – "Therefore, since we have been justified through faith, we have peace with God through our Lord

Jesus Christ, through whom we have gained access by faith into this grace in which we now stand."

Romans, 10:9–10 – "That if you confess with your mouth, 'Jesus is Lord,' and believe in your heart that God raised him from the dead, you will be saved. For it is with your heart that you believe and are justified, and it is with your mouth that you confess and are saved."

Isaiah, 26:3 – "You will keep him in perfect peace whose mind is steadfast, because he trusts in you."

Romans, 8:9 – "You, however, are controlled not by the sinful nature but by the Spirit, if the Spirit of God lives in you. And if anyone does not have the Spirit of Christ, he does not belong to Christ."

Joshua, 24:15 – "But as for me and my house, we will serve the Lord."

Galatians, 5:22 – "But the fruit of the Spirit is love, joy, peace, patience, kindness, goodness, faithfulness, gentleness and self-control."

Matthew, 5:9 – "Blessed are the peacemakers, for they will be called sons of God."

3rd John, 1:11 – "Dear friend do not imitate what is evil but what is good. Anyone who does what is good is from God. Anyone who does what is evil has not seen God."

Proverbs, 3:5–6 – "Trust in the Lord with all your heart and lean not on your own understanding; in all your ways acknowledge him, and he will make your paths straight."

"Blessed are the peacemakers, for they will be called sons of God"
(Matthew 5:9 NIV).

About the Author

The author is a practicing mediator whose work is used to train and facilitate disputes for the United States Postal Service, county court systems, churches, individuals, and other community entities and organizations. The author's experience as a restorative facilitator provides privileges to serve as a surrogate parent, mentor, and teacher.

Applying her educational background and training—master's degree in management; certificates in Family Dynamics; Advanced Transformative Mediation; Bible-based Mediation; Public Policy Dispute Resolution from the University of Texas School of Law, and Child Protective Service Mediation along with being a member of the Better Business Bureau's National Panel of Consumer Arbitrators, the author's greatest passion is inspiring others to inspire others. The author was born in Pine Bluff, Arkansas, and her hobbies are writing, singing and golfing.

THANK YOU FOR SHARING MY JOURNEY

Afterword

Dear Partner in Peace,

Thank you for allowing me to share my journey with you. I trust that something in this text has inspired you to be all that you can by seeking God's grace and guidance in your life. I want to further encourage you by asking you to assess your life right where you are at this moment. Are you experiencing rejection, hurt, bitterness, or pain because of what you believe someone else caused? If so, start now by trusting God to bring you through whatever your sorrow might be.

You can start by turning your stumbling blocks into stepping stones by a change in your desires, attitude, and perceptions. Understanding why you are experiencing your trials will help you through them. First, know that God is in complete control of everything. "The eyes of the Lord are in every place, keeping watch on the evil and the good" (Proverbs 15:3, the Gideon's). God sometimes allows us to experience adversities in our lives in order to equip us for His work. Remember trials are for a reason and season, and Romans, 8:28 teaches that: "And we know that all things work together for good to those who love God, to those who are called according to His purpose." We further learn from Scripture that "No temptation has overtaken you except such as is common to man; but God is faithful, who will not allow you to be tempted beyond what you are able, but with the temptation will also make the way of escape, that you may be able to bear it" (1 Corinthians, 10:10).

The apostle Paul was humbled by a thorn in his side. "Concerning this, he said, 'I pleaded with the Lord three times that it might depart from me', and He said to me, 'My grace is sufficient for you, for my strength is made perfect in weakness.'" 2nd Corinthians, 12:8-9.

Do you have pride, an unforgiving heart, or a desire for self-exaltation? Any of these stumbling blocks could be cause for trials in your life. As you make each stumbling block a stepping stone, use it to step over your hurt and pain, knowing and trusting God that you are being prepared for a greater work. Remember that leaving room for the opinions of others does not mean you are giving your stamp of approval. It only shows that you are big enough to respect others without denying them the right to speak their opinions, and without giving up your beliefs unless facts show otherwise. You have the power and privilege to make personal choices; you can give it to others or keep and control it in order to help others and yourself. You are not responsible for the acts of others, but are responsible for your own actions and reactions.

If you are currently in a dispute or encounter one in the future, try using your restorative conferencing skills to resolve your issue. Remain careful to respect the opinions of others; examine the claim to determine facts; and look for ways to acknowledge the positive efforts of your opponent. I wish you joy, peace, and grace as you travel your daily restorative journey.

Your partner in peace,
Edna Fenceroy

References

Leslie Marmon Silko, *Epigraph to Ceremony* (1977).

Speculum Volume 68, James H. Morey, "Peter Comestor, Biblical Paraphrase and the Medieval Popular Bible," http://en.wikimedia.org/wiki/parahase and http://changingminds.org/techniques/body_language.htm.

Watzlawick, Weakland, and Fisch (1974), "Gentle Art of Reframing," Internet.

ABC News article dated April 2, 2009, "Teen Commits Suicide Due to Bullying: Parents Sue School for Son's Death."

Versions of the Holy Bible: New International Version, the Gideons, New American Standard Translation, the One-Year Bible, the New Student Bible, and James King Version.

Authors Sameer Hinduja, PhD, and Justin W. Patchin, PhD, "Activities for Teens."

CNN.com website, August 24, 2010, "3 Colombian Teens on Facebook hit List Killed in Past 10 Days."

Emotional Intelligence, Daniel Goleman, page 289.

Oxford English Dictionary

Webster Universal Unabridged Dictionary, second edition.

ChangingMinds.org.

http://changingminds.org/techniques/body/body_language.htm.

Merriam-Webster Intermediate Dictionary.

Wisconsin Restorative Justice Program.

"Information for Friends and Family" literature revised, January 13, 2010, Ely Lilly and Company, Indianapolis, Indiana, 46285, USA.

"How much better to get wisdom than gold, to choose understanding rather than silver" (Proverbs 16:16, NIV).

NOTES